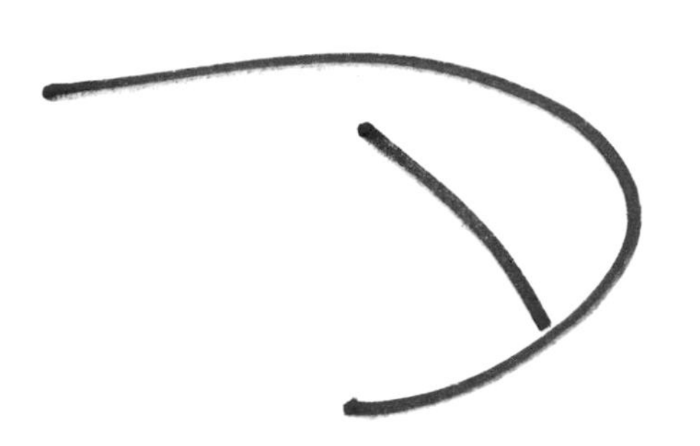

BASEBALL
SUPERSTARS

Derek Jeter

Hank Aaron

Ty Cobb

Lou Gehrig

Derek Jeter

Randy Johnson

Mike Piazza

Kirby Puckett

Jackie Robinson

Ichiro Suzuki

Bernie Williams

BASEBALL SUPERSTARS

Derek Jeter

Clifford W. Mills

DEREK JETER

Chelsea House
An imprint of Infobase Publishing
132 West 31st Street
New York NY 10001

Library of Congress Cataloging-in-Publication Data
Mills, Cliff, 1947-
Derek Jeter / Clifford W. Mills.
p. cm. — (Baseball superstars)
Includes bibliographical references and index.
ISBN-13: 978-0-7910-9422-8 (hardcover)
ISBN-10: 0-7910-9422-7 (hardcover)
1. Jeter, Derek, 1974—Juvenile literature. 2. Baseball players—United States—Biography—Juvenile literature. I. Title. II. Series.
GV865.J48M55 2007
796.357092—dc22
[B] 2007005913

Chelsea House books are available at special discounts when purchased in bulk quantities for businesses, associations, institutions, or sales promotions. Please call our Special Sales Department in New York at (212) 967-8800 or (800) 322-8755.

You can find Chelsea House on the World Wide Web at http://www.chelseahouse.com

Series design by Erik Lindstrom
Cover design by Ben Peterson

Printed in the United States of America

Bang EJB 10 9 8 7 6 5 4 3 2 1

This book is printed on acid-free paper.

All links and Web addresses were checked and verified to be correct at the time of publication. Because of the dynamic nature of the Web, some addresses and links may have changed since publication and may no longer be valid.

CONTENTS

In the Canyon of Heroes

People began to arrive in Lower Manhattan even before dawn, wanting to position themselves for a good view. Some were young and skipping school on this Tuesday in autumn. Some were older and taking the morning off from work. Some were retired, and some were not even old enough to walk. They all had one thing in common: They were all waiting in excitement for a glimpse of their newest heroes. It was October 29, 1996, and it was a day to celebrate: A few days earlier, the New York Yankees had won the World Series for the first time in 18 years, and millions of fans were ready for a party.

When the sun rose over the East River, the growing crowd of people felt warmer, and they could see the sun gleaming off the tall buildings that tower over Broadway from Battery Park

The New York Yankees celebrated their 1996 World Series victory with a parade on October 29 in the Canyon of Heroes in Lower Manhattan. More than 3 million fans crowded Broadway and surrounding streets to honor the team. The World Series win was the first for the Yankees in 18 years.

to City Hall Park. These skyscrapers form the world's greatest financial district, and on this day the highest and mightiest buildings were the twin towers of the World Trade Center. They seemed to keep watch over the crowd.

This section of Broadway is called the "Canyon of Heroes" because it has been a main parade route for American heroes for more than 100 years. President Theodore Roosevelt (on June 18, 1910) and Prime Minister Winston Churchill of Great Britain (March 14, 1946) were cheered along this same route for their world leadership. Charles Lindbergh (June 13, 1927), Amelia Earhart (June 20, 1932), and Howard Hughes (June 15, 1938) were recognized for their extraordinary and brave solo flights across the Atlantic Ocean and around the world. John Glenn (March 1, 1962) and the Apollo 11 astronauts Neil Armstrong, Edwin Aldrin, and Michael Collins (August 13, 1969) had been through the canyon, marking their achievements in space flight.

All had been showered with "ticker tape," a special paper that fed stock-quotation machines. On this day, long after the advent of computers on Wall Street, ticker tape had been replaced by confetti—torn office paper, newspaper bits, shredded phone books, and computer printouts, hundreds of tons of it.

Two of the New York Yankees players, Jim Leyritz and Derek Jeter, decided to skip the team bus from Yankee Stadium and take the subway. As they got closer to where the parade was to begin at 11:30 A.M., they began to notice just how packed and noisy the subway cars were. Some fans recognized Jeter, the sensational rookie shortstop, and began to call out to him. When he and Leyritz tried to leave the subway at Battery Park, a small stampede of fans made them wonder if they would be able to get up the subway stairs and out into the park. They breathed a sigh of relief when they climbed onto the 18-foot-high (5.5-meter-high) floats that would take them down the Canyon of Heroes.

JETERMANIA

The 22-year-old Yankees shortstop was used to being cheered, but he had never experienced this kind of crushing adoration before. Few on Earth have. As the parade began, the other Yankee players began to notice the signs being carried by young women, signs that read, "Nothing is sweeter than Derek Jeter." They started to tease the rookie. Hundreds of love letters came

YANKEE STADIUM

Yankee Stadium is the grand and famous home stadium of the New York Yankees. The stadium, which is at East 161st Street and River Avenue in the Bronx, New York City, opened with wild celebration on April 18, 1923, and reopened on April 15, 1976, after an extensive three-year renovation. It was the first baseball park to be named a "stadium" (instead of "field," "park," or "grounds") because it contained an element that stadiums in ancient Greece had: a running track. The track served as a "warning track" for outfielders about to run into the outfield wall, a feature that is now standard on baseball fields but was unheard of then.

The field was not symmetrical: The middle of left field was 460 feet (140 meters) from the center of home plate, and the middle of right field was only 350 feet (107 meters) away. Some baseball historians believe this was done because the famous Yankee player Babe Ruth was left-handed and therefore could hit more home runs to right field as he pulled the ball with his powerful swing. So, the legend goes, Yankee Stadium was built to suit Ruth's swing. Others dispute this idea and point to early maps of the building site. They argue that the building was designed simply to fit the existing plot of land. Making right field larger

flying at Jeter from all directions, resulting in more teasing. Darryl Strawberry, a Yankee who had played for the New York Mets when they won the 1986 World Series, had participated in the Mets' parade through these same canyons. He said later in an interview, "The Mets got like 2 million people; the Yankees had 3 million. The extra million were for Jeter, all those 13- and 14-year-old girls."

would have meant building a "Green Monster," like the high wall found in Boston's Fenway Park.

Left-center field soon came to be called "Death Valley" because many balls hit there were caught, even though they would have been hits or home runs in other parks. Another Yankee great, Joe DiMaggio, batted right-handed and hit many long balls to left field. Many fans believe that he lost more home runs because of his home ballpark than any player in major-league history. In 2005, Alex Rodriguez became the first right-handed Yankee to hit 40 home runs in a season since 1937, the year that DiMaggio hit 46. The fences have been moved several times since 1973, and currently the middle of left field is 379 feet (116 meters) from home plate, and the middle of right field is 353 feet (108 meters) away. The left-handed favor is still there but is not as strong as it once was. "Death Valley" has been tamed and populated with seats filled with rabid Yankee fans.

The team broke ground in 2006 on a new Yankee Stadium, which is being built across the street from the present stadium. The new ballpark will open in 2009. The design re-creates some of the original stadium's features, and the field dimensions will be the same.

People began to scream "Derek, Derek" when he came into view, and the crowds surged forward to be closer to him. One woman watching from her office in the financial district had seen these parades before. This one was different. She told reporters: "I don't know what happened to us. We saw the Yankee floats, and we saw Derek waving, and he flashes us that smile . . . and every one of us completely lost it. Half the women on my floor were so exhausted afterward, they skipped work and just went home. It was pure insanity. We loved it."

People seeing Derek Jeter for the first time often notice the same attributes: At 6-foot-3 (190.5 centimeters), he is taller than he looks on television. He is friendly and poised, and seems both shy and outgoing at the same time. His skin seems to glow and radiate warmth. He laughs suddenly, then turns serious for a moment, then seems playful again. His smile is genuine and makes others smile. His eyes are a vivid green; he seems to notice all that is going on around him but is not nervous or anxious. All of these traits were on display as he rode with his teammates during his first, but not last, parade as a New York Yankees World Champion.

A new breed of fan was born, the Jeterettes. A new term came into use, *Jetermania.* New York City does not swoon over a baseball player very often. The city and its fans had embraced Babe Ruth, Jackie Robinson, Joe DiMaggio, Willie Mays, and Mickey Mantle, but they were stars who left the field long ago. The city was now in love with a new star, and it proclaimed its love for the first time on this bright October morning.

PURE REJOICING

Jeter responded to the people in the crowd. Students from the parochial school of the Nativity of the Blessed Virgin Mary Church in Queens waved at him. Their principal was Sister Mary Marguerite Torre, the sister of Yankees manager Joe Torre. John and Megan Fahy were there, a brother and sister whose parents had both been in the New York Police

Yankee players *(from left)* Cecil Fielder, Charlie Hayes, and Derek Jeter headed up Broadway on a float during the World Series parade in 1996. New York fans seemed to embrace Jeter, a rookie that year, as one of their new heroes, just as they had done with baseball stars in the past, like Babe Ruth and Joe DiMaggio.

Department and loved the Yankees. Gloria McMahan and her daughter waved to Jeter and his teammates and rejoiced that they were there for this historic moment. Many later recalled that they felt they were part of something very special, something that brought the city together.

Rudolph Giuliani, the mayor of New York City, called it "a magic time of heroic achievement," and he gave keys to the city to each of the players when they arrived at City Hall Park. The mayor also held up a case of Diet Coke and an order of ribs

team and what it could do. He was more than a championship baseball player. He was a good and caring man.

GIVING BACK: THE TURN 2 FOUNDATION IS BORN

Only a few weeks before the Yankees were to enter the playoffs in 1996, Jeter sat in the Ritz-Carlton hotel in Dearborn, Michigan. It was September 9, and the Yankees were to play the Detroit Tigers the next night. Jeter had flown in early to be with his father, Charles. He was and is very close to his father and mother, and he had not seen his father for far too long. Jeter was nearing the end of his first full season in the major leagues, and he was thinking about what he and his team had accomplished. He did not want to go out that night, preferring to eat a $12 room-service pizza with his father, so they could be alone and not be bothered by anyone.

He was suddenly overcome with a feeling that he needed to share the success he was experiencing and help others get a chance to achieve their own success. "I want to start a foundation," he said. Being with his father had awakened an impulse to give back, to honor all that his parents had given to him. His father had coached his Little League teams, and his mother had started mentoring programs for public-school students in Kalamazoo. They were both in the Parent-Teacher Association and had attended every school play, even if Derek or Sharlee was not in it. He wanted to make his parents proud of him, for something other than playing baseball. He was making $120,000 a year, a good salary but a fraction of what he would earn later. Jeter felt he had to share his wealth even before he became wealthy, just as his parents had shared with others. He writes in his autobiography about his thoughts at the time:

> You see, I've always had a great relationship with my parents and I know not everyone is fortunate enough to have that. Some people aren't even fortunate enough to have both parents active in their lives. That was the biggest factor that

Derek Jeter ran drills with the Western Michigan University softball team in January 2001 during the Turn 2 Foundation's "Nurturing Dreams" Jamboree. The event was held at the university, which is in Jeter's hometown, Kalamazoo, Michigan. During his rookie season, Jeter discussed with his father the idea of starting a foundation. Since its formation, Turn 2 has awarded more than $6 million in grants.

> motivated me to start the Turn 2 Foundation. The whole basis for it was for me to use my experiences to guide kids in the right direction by telling them why they shouldn't use drugs or alcohol. . . . I tutored other students when I was in high school and I've always had an affinity for helping underdogs. We should all give back.

His father was, as usual, careful and analytical in his response. He asked his son if he knew how much work an effective foundation would be and how much time it would take. He told Derek that he could not be casual about such an important matter. Soon, they were developing plans for what would be the Turn 2 Foundation, an organization that has raised millions of dollars for students in New York City, Kalamazoo, and Tampa, Florida, and to which Jeter devotes a good deal of his time. The foundation changed his father's life as well. Charles Jeter is now the head of it.

Professional baseball teams are made up of players with many different backgrounds, and having players who can help generate a sense of togetherness is a rare and valuable asset. Jeter is one of those players who brings a team together. Differences in race and age simply do not limit his empathy for others. He interacts easily with everyone, including fans. He has had such a strong and positive family experience that generating a family feeling within the clubhouse and with others seems to come naturally to him. Playing baseball had not just been a sport to him. It had been a way of being close to his mother, father, and sister. It had been a way of defining what a family was. Some say he was born this way. Some say he was made this way, starting from his very earliest days.

Growing Up with a Dream

Derek Sanderson Jeter was born on June 26, 1974, in Pequannock, New Jersey, not far from New York City. His family moved to North Arlington, New Jersey, not long after he was born; the town is also not too far from Manhattan but far enough away that some city dwellers would come out for its fresh air and change of scenery. His mother, Dorothy, also from New Jersey, was born in Jersey City, one of 14 children. She was raised in West Milford and was an accountant with Upjohn Pharmaceuticals when she gave birth to Derek. His father, Charles, is from Montgomery, Alabama; he and his four sisters grew up in a small apartment, cared for only by their mother, Lugenia, who cleaned houses. Charles never knew his father and must have vowed, when Derek was born, to give his new son the love and attention he never received from his own father. Charles met Dorothy in Frankfurt, Germany, in 1972, when they were both stationed there in the U.S. Army. Charles Jeter was an alcohol and drug counselor and a social worker after he left the army, and he continues such work today, especially with troubled children and teens.

JETER'S PARENTS

Jeter's parents are a study in contrasts. Dorothy is Irish and fair-skinned, with very light brown hair. She is outgoing and quick to laugh and has the assertiveness that a child among 13 others must have to get heard (and fed). Charles is African American, with short black hair and a black beard. He is thoughtful and analytical, with a soothing voice. He is slower to show emotion than his wife. Charles was a good athlete, good enough to play shortstop for Fisk University in Nashville, Tennessee. Derek would later tease him that his scrapbook of baseball accomplishments was slim, but Charles was clearly a gifted baseball player.

Dorothy and Charles were married in Tennessee in 1973. That act took a good deal of courage. When Dorothy told her parents that she was going to marry Charles, she thought they would be happy for her. Her father, however, asked if she knew the kinds of problems she would encounter from others because of intolerance of mixed-race marriages. His question disappointed Dorothy, but she was not going to be stopped, even by her father. She was in love, and no one would tell her whom she could or could not marry.

One of the most shameful parts of American history is the set of state laws that prohibited people of different ethnic backgrounds from getting married. Every state except Vermont has passed, at some point in its history, a law against miscegenation (the formal name for intermarriage or relationships between people of different ethnicities). In 1967, only six years before Jeter's parents married, the Supreme Court ruled that such laws against intermarriage were unconstitutional, saying that the freedom to marry a man or woman of another race is a basic civil right. Only in November 2000, however, did the last state, Alabama, repeal its laws banning miscegenation. As recently as 2003, 30 percent of Americans polled were still against marriage between African Americans and white people. Or, put another way, 70 percent of Americans now believe in the civil right of intermarriage.

When Derek was four years old, his family moved from North Arlington, New Jersey, to Kalamazoo, Michigan. Kalamazoo is a city of approximately 80,000 people in southwestern Michigan, midway between Detroit and Chicago. It is home to Western Michigan University and Kalamazoo College and had been a manufacturing center for windmills and automobiles. It is a diversified and important Midwestern city, and Jeter remembers it fondly as a good place to grow up.

He also remembers, however, that some people did not even try to overcome their ignorance, insecurity, and prejudice. In his autobiography, he describes several scenes related to his parents' racial differences:

> The stares often followed us into restaurants, during searches for apartments, and when my mother picked me up from an after-school program for black children. There were a lot of people who stared at me and my family when I was younger. . . . I was an innocent kid, so I couldn't understand why someone would dislike me because of my mom and my dad. How could they not like them? My parents are gracious people. I didn't really dwell on race unless someone else made it an issue because a white mother and black father is the only family that I know.

When his father went looking for an apartment in Kalamazoo, he was told by one superintendent that none were available. When his mother went to the same apartment building, she was welcomed and offered one immediately. When both his father and mother came to sign the lease and pick up the keys, the superintendent was shocked. Antidiscrimination housing laws have been strengthened since the 1970s, so at least some of the blatant practices used against the Jeters would be prosecuted today.

Dorothy and Charles Jeter were stronger than the prejudice they faced. They shielded their children from as much as they could, and, more important, taught their children coping skills that prevented problems from getting bigger. Many who know Derek well say he uses his biracial nature to his advantage, appealing to blacks, whites, Hispanics, and people of all races and backgrounds. He is often compared to golfer Tiger Woods in this respect; both men have felt blessed by their parents' gifts to them, gifts that include their physical talents and their emotional strength. Jeter, like Woods, credits his parents with teaching him some very important lessons. In his autobiography, he writes about his biracial heritage:

> I've talked to people who are the products of biracial parents and who have identity problems. They don't know who they are, what they are, or how they should act. I never had those problems and still don't. I think my parents prepared me for that. I was and still am proud of who I am. . . . I've had people ask me if I was Italian, Puerto Rican, Indian, white, black. . . . If someone mistakes me for being something that I am not, I don't consider that a slight because I can identify with these people.

WALKING INTO YANKEE STADIUM FOR THE FIRST TIME

Every summer as a child, Derek was sent back to New Jersey to spend time with his grandparents. They lived on a lake, and Derek loved being with them. His grandmother, Dorothy Connors, was a Yankees fan and always had been since she was old enough to sit next to her father and eat crackers as they listened to Yankee games on the radio. Grandmother Connors loved Babe Ruth most of all, and she waited in line for hours on a hot day in August 1948 to pay her respects during a memorial service for him. She knew all about Yankee history and was waiting for the chance to share her stories with a willing listener. She and Derek began to watch games on television. Before long, she had instilled a love of baseball in her grandson, passing her affection and knowledge from one generation to another.

Derek must have been a handful for his grandparents. He used to wake his grandmother as early as 6 A.M. to play catch. She soon noticed that Derek threw the ball harder than his cousins did. As he grew a little older, he was almost knocking her down with his throws. She saw early on that Derek had a rare natural ability.

One bright and beautiful day in the summer of 1980, Grandmother Connors told Derek that they would be going to Yankee Stadium to watch a game. That day would change his life. Neither Jeter nor his grandmother remembers who won or even which team the Yankees played, but both recall Derek's reaction to Yankee Stadium. The field seemed bigger than anything he had ever seen. The swept dirt and emerald-green grass must have carried him to another world.

His uncle bought him a Yankees cap, one he wore every day for the rest of the summer. An ambition seemed to awaken within Derek, a combination of wanting to be part of something as big as the Yankees and wanting to win at whatever he did. He now had a goal, but one large enough and distant enough to be called a dream. His goal, his dream, changed both him and the course of Yankees history. Derek returned to Kalamazoo later that summer a different boy. He writes about somehow now knowing what he wanted to do with his life:

> I walked along our thick carpet, past the pictures of my grandparents on the hallway walls and into my parents'

The outside of Yankee Stadium in the Bronx is pictured in this photograph from the early 1980s. In 1980, when Derek Jeter was six years old, his grandmother took him to his first Yankees game at the stadium. After that game, Derek had a dream—to play shortstop for the Yankees.

bedroom. I announced that I was going to play for the Yankees. They were already in their pajamas, but they patiently listened to what their skinny son with the wavy brown hair and green eyes had said, and then told me the type of thing I was aching to hear. They told me that I could do anything I wanted in life if I worked hard enough and stayed dedicated to it. . . . My parents could have gently put me off and told me to go to sleep that night, but instead were receptive to my dream and talked about what it would take to achieve such a difficult goal.

JETER'S COMPETITIVE NATURE

Having parents who did not discourage his dream was one part of the formula in the making of this baseball superstar. There was another ingredient. Some psychologists have said that three kinds of personalities exist. The first is a controlling person, someone who likes to tell others what to do. The second is a dependent person, one who always relies on others. The third is a competitive person, someone who needs to win. There is little doubt what kind of personality Jeter has. He is competitive and has been as long as anyone could remember.

One of Derek's earliest memories is of watching the TV show *The Price Is Right* with his father. He was probably four or five years old. The contestants were asked to guess the price of a toaster. Derek guessed $400. His father did not laugh but guessed the exact amount, $20. His father never belittled his guesses, or his ideas, but quietly stressed that a person will have advantages and disadvantages in playing any game. You must never use your disadvantages as an excuse when you lose, his father explained. Being too young to know the right answer was a disadvantage but should not be an excuse.

Charles Jeter would beat young Derek at checkers, Scrabble, pool, basketball, and every other game they played. He never let Derek win. He knew that, when Derek finally did win at some game, the victory would mean more. And winning was a goal that Derek began to crave. His competitive nature was soon going to have an outlet.

JOINING LITTLE LEAGUE

Baseball became one of the games he could win. Derek signed up for T-ball and for Little League. No one videotaped his first day of tryouts for the Westwood Little League in Kalamazoo, but his father later recalled that Derek looked right at home. He loved Opening Day. Hundreds of fans packed the stands while all the teams marched onto the field. Derek liked to play in front of these crowds. He reminded himself that all he had to do was play the game the way he played in his own backyard and with Grandmother Connors.

In Little League, what first sets a player apart is his or her throwing ability. How fast and how far players can throw a ball determine how soon coaches and other parents notice them. Derek could throw the ball harder and faster than almost any other child his age. To throw a ball fast, all the neurons and muscles in the arm and shoulders have to fire in an almost perfect sequence. The body has to know how to coordinate

☆ ☆ ☆ ☆ ☆ ☆

LITTLE LEAGUE

Little League Baseball is played in more than 100 countries and every state in America. On an average summer day, some 400,000 children are playing on almost 12,000 fields in the United States alone. The nonprofit organization was founded in 1939 by Carl Stotz and his friends as a three-team league in Williamsport, Pennsylvania, then still a lumber center on the Susquehanna River with several millionaires living in Victorian mansions. Little League's current headquarters are directly across the river from the site of the original league.

Roughly 80 percent of all major-league players started in Little League. They played in "little leagues" that are divided into six divisions based on the ages of the children: T-Ball, Minors, Little, Junior, Senior, and Big. "Little League" is generally for players age 9 to 12, but other ages are included in some leagues. Each league must play at least 12 games in a season, and the winners of the regional playoffs go to Williamsport for the Little League World Series, now shown on ESPN. Tournaments are played in the United States, Canada, Europe, Latin America, and Asia. Winners of the Little League World Series have included teams from many countries. Some fans think that international

several complex motions. Derek seemed to have been born with that ability or at least to have developed it at a very early age. A strong arm would have meant that his first Little League coaches would have wanted to make him a pitcher, and indeed Derek was a pitcher in at least some games.

Jeter's father had been a shortstop, and Jeter wanted to be like his father. He wanted to play shortstop. A shortstop plays between second and third base, and must have quickness and a good arm. He or she has to move quickly from side to side to

teams have an advantage since they often draw players from a larger geographic district than American teams.

Visitors to the series have included Jackie Robinson, Mickey Mantle, President George W. Bush and his father, George H.W. Bush. Actors Kevin Costner and Tom Selleck and writer John Grisham have enjoyed games. Grisham even wrote a screenplay about an overage Little Leaguer who fools everyone and pitches in the World Series. The story came true.

Danny Almonte led his Bronx, New York, team to the 2001 Little League World Series, during which he threw a perfect game (giving up no hits, no walks, and no runs). His 75-mile-per-hour (121-kilometer-per-hour) fastball was almost unhittable. A reporter found that his birth certificate was almost certainly falsified and that Almonte was 14 and not 12 in the 2001 series. He was therefore ineligible. His team lost to Apopka, Florida, which in turn lost the championship to the Japan All-Stars. Danny now lives in Miami, Florida, and is considered a major-league pitching prospect. His fastball is up to 90 miles per hour (145 kilometers per hour), but the high point of his baseball career may still have been his 2001 perfect game.

cover the widest area in the infield. A shortstop also needs to be able to throw out a runner from "the hole," the space behind shortstop almost into left field. Derek could make plays "in the hole" almost as soon as he joined Little League. He was quick, and he could throw far and fast.

Most world-class athletes have extraordinary capabilities in any or all of three physical areas: muscular strength, vision, and reaction time. Derek was blessed with good vision and an ability to react very quickly to what was happening around him. He worked on his muscular strength when he got to high school and continues to work on it almost every day.

DEVELOPING SKILLS EARLY

Another skill that gets noticed early is how forcefully a player swings the bat. By the time he joined Little League, Derek had already developed his batting stance into a smaller version of the stance he would take later—a crouch, bending sharply at the waist, with his right knee bent and left foot lifted. He held his bat high above his shoulders, wiggling it back and forth as if it were bait trying to attract the pitch. When he swung, he exploded in a controlled fury, even at this young age. His bat moved quickly through the strike zone, in a whipping motion. As a result, the ball flew off the bat. His father can take some credit for that swing: He was Derek's Little League coach during some of the years he played. The Yankees videotaped Jeter's swing from 1992 to 1999 and found little difference from the first taping to the last. He seems to have found his groove in his swing at a very young age and remained in that groove.

A baseball player also needs running speed and quickness in moving left and right from a dead stop. The quickest runners get noticed in Little League. Derek was extremely fast. When he hit the ball, he was a blur leaving the batter's box and heading to first base, an instant starter who reached full speed in very few steps.

In the on-deck circle, Derek Jeter warmed up during the first inning of a 2003 game against the Chicago Cubs. Jeter's distinctive batting stance—crouched with his right knee bent and his left leg lifted—was already developed when he was playing Little League as a child.

The goal in baseball, above all else, is to score runs, and speed helps. Jeter loved the feeling of scoring a run right from the start of his playing days. Few players have scored as many runs as Jeter in the major leagues, and his focus on running bases to score runs started when he was in Little League.

Another crucial skill is fielding the ball, which requires several abilities. First, a player has to see the ball as it comes off the bat and judge instantly (in less than a third of a second) where it is going. The player must move quickly to that spot and watch the ball go into the glove. Then, the player needs to transfer the ball from glove to hand and throw the ball to the correct base in little time. Unlike throwing, running, and swinging, the fielding motion is a skill that needs to be learned through constant repetition. Fielding is not as natural as running, throwing, and swinging. Jeter admits that he has had games when he prayed that the ball would not be hit to him. When it is, he sometimes has the mentality of a hockey goalie—he just wants to keep the ball from going past him. In Little League and all the way through his baseball career, fielding is the one skill that seems to make Derek less comfortable and less than extraordinary. He is mortal after all. Part of his game does not come naturally.

LEARNING IMPORTANT LESSONS EARLY

One day Derek came to his father and said he would not be at Little League practice. His father, then the coach, asked why. Derek said he wanted to go fishing with one of his friends. He had never been fishing and wanted to try a new activity. His father replied that, if Derek went fishing and skipped practice, he could not start the next game. To not practice was to let down his team, and Derek would have to choose between fishing and baseball. Derek went to practice and has not missed a required practice at any level of baseball since. So, there is another ingredient to superstardom: focus and commitment. He participates fully in every practice, every game, every at-bat, every pitch. Even in the dugout, he watches every play and every player. His concentration is intense.

During one of his Little League games, Derek had a moment at the plate that he still remembers. He swung at and missed the first two pitches, neither of which was a strike. He watched the third pitch come in, did not swing, and heard the words every player dreads: "Strike three!" He fumed later to his father that the umpire made a bad call. The pitch was not a strike. His father listened carefully, then asked Derek why he did not focus more on the two pitches he missed. "Control what you can control." The lesson was a crucial one for Derek, on two levels.

Derek Jeter congratulated Jason Giambi after Giambi hit a two-run homer in an April 2006 game against the Toronto Blue Jays. One day when Derek was in Little League, he was so frustrated after a lopsided loss that he did not participate with his team in the customary closing cheers. His father scolded him and reminded him that he should always support his teammates. Today, Jeter is generally the first one out of the Yankee dugout to congratulate a fellow player.

First, he needed to reduce his swings at bad pitches. Second, he had to focus on his performance, not on how others might be holding him back.

Finally, there is yet one more lesson that Derek incorporated early on, again from his father. Before his father was his coach, Derek's Little League team had suffered a one-sided loss and Derek was frustrated. He refused to get up and shake the hands of the other team's players after the game. He would not join in the customary closing cheers and stayed on the bench, away from his teammates. Derek's father was watching, and he was embarrassed. He gave Derek a quick but stern lecture: If he did not learn how to lose gracefully and support his own teammates, he should take up an individual sport like golf or tennis. If his son wanted all the praise or blame, then a team sport like baseball was not for him. Derek listened. To this day, he is almost always the first player out of the Yankee dugout to congratulate a teammate who has hit a home run.

FIRST PRACTICE FIELDS: THE EARLY FIELDS OF DREAMS

When Jeter first joined Little League, his family was living at the Mount Royal Townhouse Complex in Kalamazoo. Jammed in among the carports, apartments, and parking spaces was a small grassy area about 150 feet (46 meters) from Derek's townhouse. It was more of a hillside slope than a baseball field, but it became the first field of Derek's dreams. Derek's best friend, Doug Biro, would ride his bike to meet at "Jeter's Hill" for a game of catch or a real game if more than four people showed up. When Derek was not at school or asleep, he was at "Jeter's Hill" playing and talking baseball. He became the Pied Piper of the townhouse development, and more and more kids flocked to be with him. Derek and Doug challenged each other and shared their dreams. Doug wanted to be a professional golfer. Everyone knew what Derek wanted to be. Doug and Derek still talk all the time.

When Derek was 10 years old, his family moved into their first real house. It was a cozy yellow home with a small front yard and a slightly bigger backyard. The house had one major advantage: It was directly behind the playing fields of Kalamazoo Central High School. When Derek shattered a picture window in the new home on their first day there, the entire family jumped the small fence behind their house and started to play on the high school field. Sharlee had been born four years earlier, but she was soon old enough to play outfield when Derek batted and bat when Derek played outfield. His father pitched, his mother played infield and outfield, and the family played for hours on end. Neighbors remember driving by the field at twilight and seeing the entire Jeter family still out in the distance, laughing and playing and encouraging one another.

"Some people go to the movies for fun. We went to the field. It was part of being close," Sharlee Jeter said in a 1999 *USA Today* article.

Derek would tease his father that he was too slow, or too old. His mother would tease them both, saying they were slower than Sharlee. His father would say that he was better at fielding ground balls and that maybe it was not too late for him to get to the major leagues. His father and mother both delighted in throwing Wiffle-ball pitches that Derek had trouble handling. They threw some nasty curveballs, and Derek and Sharlee had to stay sharp and keep their eyes on the darting and sinking ball. The family had always been close, but now their bond grew even stronger. Jeter would remember those days on the Central High field as some of the happiest of his life.

Getting the Call

Baseball was not Derek Jeter's whole life. He was an excellent student at his elementary school, St. Augustine's, and teachers there fondly remember his interest in many subjects. He expressed himself well in his school reports, was a fast reader, and worked hard. He made friends easily, including one friend he met in eighth grade who would become his first girlfriend, Marisa Novara. She remains a close friend to this day, and when Jeter has a game in Chicago against the White Sox, he always tries to see her for lunch. They talk about everything except baseball.

JETER PARENTING STYLES: THE FIRST CONTRACT

Derek graduated from St. Augustine School in 1988, and his yearbook spells out his goal to become a New York Yankee.

Setting goals had become second nature, but that practice would soon be taken to a whole new level. Two weeks before he entered Kalamazoo Central High School, the school just out his back door, his father and mother sat him down for a Sunday night conference. They presented him with a contract that they signed and wanted him to sign. The contract spelled out the goals they expected him to achieve during his first high school year—grade-point average, athletic accomplishments, obeying curfews, everything. "No alcohol and drugs" and "Respect girls" were two contract items. Jeter's father had seen parents use contracts with troubled teenagers who had made serious mistakes. He reasoned that a contract might be effective before mistakes were made. Derek did not agree with every clause, but he did sign the contract after some discussion.

Some parents are authoritarian, imposing standards on their children and punishing them if they do not live up to those standards. Their children may grow up with lower self-esteem if they do not feel in control. Other parents are permissive, letting their children do pretty much what they want. Their children can be impulsive and undisciplined. Derek's parents were a third kind. They were authoritative. They set standards and goals, but they encouraged discussion and creative thinking about how to meet those objectives. Children of these kinds of parents tend to be more self-controlled and independent, and have higher self-esteem. In his autobiography, Jeter writes about his parents:

> I wasn't allowed to drink, smoke, or do drugs. My parents told me they were opposed to premarital sex, but if I decided to have sex, I should use the proper birth control protection. . . . They told me if I was ever at a party or around a group of people "drinking and drugging," as my father used to say, they would come and pick me up, and they would ask no questions. But if they found out I had been with people who

Derek Jeter and his father, Charles, hugged during a presentation before a Yankees game on Father's Day in 2005. Jeter's parents always taught him to pursue his dreams. Charles and Dorothy Jeter were authoritative parents yet they also encouraged discussion with their children about their goals.

used drugs and alcohol and had not left immediately, they would ask *lots* of questions.

Derek had some goals set for him, but he was encouraged to set goals of his own. One day during his first year at Kalamazoo Central, he opened *USA Today* and read an article about Tyler Houston, of Las Vegas, Nevada, who had just been named "High School Player of the Year." Tyler's picture was in the form of a baseball card. Without hesitating, Derek set a goal. In three years, he would become the "High School Player of the Year." Looking at Derek, many people might have said that his goal was unrealistic. He was only 14, tall and thin, and not yet strong. He was not living in a warm climate where he could practice all year. He vowed, however, that he would work to make himself better and stronger. He would lift weights, practice harder, and learn more.

When he told his mother about the article and his plan, she said it was an excellent goal. She encouraged him in exactly the right way at exactly the right moment. Derek's mother knew him well, and she knew he was gifted physically and mentally. She loved her son's gifts, and she knew how to help him share them with others.

GETTING BIGGER AND BETTER

Some boys mature earlier than others. The early bloomers have a growth spurt before the average boys. Child psychologists have noticed a pattern among boys who mature early. They are more likely to excel at athletics, be more popular in school, be more poised with girls, and be more relaxed than other boys. They have less conflict with their parents and siblings and have fewer run-ins with teachers.

Derek had his growth spurt early. He was nearly 6 feet tall at 14 years old, and 6 feet 2 inches at 16. He fits the pattern child psychologists have noticed. He was popular, poised, close to his parents, and liked by teachers. He was relaxed and not afraid of what might happen to him. So, he was lucky enough to have the right parents and the right genes. He was also lucky enough to have a well-organized baseball system in his hometown.

Don Zomer, a Kalamazoo high school baseball coach, remembers that he heard about a fantastic player in Little League, someone named Derek Jeter. He did not think about the player again until he saw him for the first time, when Jeter was in the Mickey Mantle League at age 14. He told a reporter, "In Mickey Mantle, they had him playing third base. He was an instant star. He's always played one step ahead of where his age group was, and he still does." Soon Derek moved up to the next level, the Connie Mack League, for youths up to 18. His team, called the Maroons, played almost 75 games. So, for the first time, Derek had plenty of playing experience during the summer. He was only 15, but he was playing against older athletes. The level of play in the Kalamazoo leagues was very high, and even then Derek was a star.

Zomer became his coach at Kalamazoo Central, and he soon noticed that Derek hit balls that many high school players just could not handle. Derek's throws were approaching 90 miles per hour (145 kilometers per hour), almost unheard of for someone his age. What impressed Zomer the most, however, was that Derek did not act like a star. He worked hard, cared about his teammates, and thought about how the team could get better, not just about how Derek Jeter could improve. "He was always focused on the team," Zomer remembered.

BEING SCOUTED

Zomer was not the only baseball expert who had heard about this amazing young player, and by Derek's junior year at Kalamazoo Central, professional baseball scouts were attending almost every game. Baseball scouts use a grading system to judge the potential of a major-league prospect. They assess fielding, hitting, throwing, and base running, along with other qualities that are harder to measure, like attitude and work ethic. A 50 is a good score. Some scouts had Jeter at 55 or higher. Some even thought he would be the number-one pick in the overall amateur draft, which included college and high school players. Almost all of the 28 major-league teams were tracking him. He had been a "follow," a scout's term for a prospect of interest who is 15 or 16. Now he was a real prospect.

Don Zomer, who was Derek Jeter's high school baseball coach at Kalamazoo Central, stood next to a figure of Jeter that was part of an interactive exhibit at Madame Tussauds wax museum in New York. "He's always played one step ahead of where his age group was, and he still does," Zomer said about Jeter.

Derek's batting average at the end of his junior year was .557, a school record. The scouts, however, were aware of the aluminum bat factor. All high school players use an aluminum bat, while all major-league players use a wooden one. The aluminum bat allows for greater bat speed since it is lighter, and the ball travels almost 20 percent farther. So, a 400-foot (122-meter) home run with an aluminum bat may only be a 320-foot (98-meter) out with a wooden bat. Scouts also look at whether a shortstop can throw a ball from the edge of the

BASEBALL SCOUTS

The 1994 movie *The Scout* stars actor Albert Brooks as a Yankees baseball scout and Brendan Fraser as a great, undiscovered pitcher playing in small parks in Mexico. The movie calls attention to the life of a baseball scout: endless driving to lonely, far-off places, fast food for every meal, cheap motels instead of a home, few personal relationships, and getting scooped by other scouts. The movie's happy ending, with Fraser's character starring in Yankee Stadium, seems to make all the sacrifices worthwhile.

Scouts perform a crucial function. They rate players from around the country. Some use a rating system from 2 to 8; some use a 20-to-80 scale. A 2- or a 20-rated player is not worth a second look. An 8 or an 80 is for the best amateur players in the country. Anyone above a 4 or a 40 is considered a major-league prospect. Players other than pitchers are rated on arm strength, running speed, fielding ability, the ability to hit, and the ability to hit with power. Pitching prospects are graded on their fastball, curveball, slider, and other pitches. Finally, a "player's makeup" is rated: How much does the prospect want to improve, want to learn, and want to win? Does he have "baseball smarts"? How

outfield grass to first base, almost 150 feet (46 meters), without the ball sinking before it gets to first. The scouts rate the prospect higher if the long throw doesn't "die," especially if it hits the glove with a distinct popping sound. Derek's rating meant that he easily passed most of the tests.

PLAYING THROUGH PAIN

Just when it seemed as if nothing could stop him, Derek had the biggest scare of his young baseball life. Near the beginning

mature is he? Can he adjust to being away from home? Can he adapt to long bus rides, bad lighting, and poor playing conditions in front of only a few heckling fans? Will the player likely get stronger and bigger?

Scouting has changed. Many years ago, a team might divide the country into a few geographical areas and have one scout for each area. Each scout would use friends and acquaintances as "bird dogs" to go to smaller high school games to look for prospects. They would all share their notes, sometimes on coffee-stained scraps of paper. Now, computerized databases, scouting combines like the Major League Scouting Bureau, international training facilities, and sophisticated measuring techniques take some of the guesswork out of the process. But not all. Personal judgments are still needed.

The scouting process is very democratic and open to all. If someone wants to share information on a potential prospect, he or she can send a DVD, a videotape, pictures, and statistics to the Major League Scouting Bureau, 3500 Porsche Way, Suite 100, Ontario, CA 91764.

of his senior-year season in 1992, his team played Portage Central on a snowy and cold April day. Forty scouts were in the stands, and they all knew that Derek had hit three home runs in his first nine at-bats that season. Derek hit a slow ground ball and hustled down the wet, slick baseline toward first base. As always, he wanted a hit and was willing to run as fast as he could. When he got to the base, he hit the bag off center and toppled in a heap, clutching his ankle. He was in so much pain that he thought he had broken it. The people in the stands became completely quiet, and he saw all of his dreams suddenly threatened. His best friend, Doug Biro, raced over; Derek could not even speak. As he was helped off the field by his father, the silence in the stands scared him.

Doctors told him he would be out six to eight weeks—most of the season. Even though his ankle was not broken, he might have been better off if it had been. Derek had a severe sprain, and some ankle sprains can take longer to heal than breaks. All of his skills and all of his coaching could not help him now. Only one thing would get him through: his will to succeed. He knew he had to find a way to play. After missing only three games, Derek returned as a designated hitter, wearing an ankle brace and high-top cleats. He could barely run, but he soon took the field. He could not push off his ankle when he was hitting. Derek hit only one home run in the next 50 at-bats. Yet, he willed himself to play harder and to play in pain. When many players would have quit, he did not. He needed to succeed now, in his senior year, or the scouts could possibly overlook him. His batting average dropped, but at .508 he was still one of the best players in the country.

GETTING DRAFTED

One of his major goals from three years earlier, being the *USA Today* "High School Player of the Year," became a reality. He was overjoyed. All of his work had paid off. Swinging the bat 1,000 times a day in his garage at a ball hung from the ceiling had helped. Repetition had led to an almost automatic hitting reflex. Fielding ground balls over and over had helped him become comfortable and even relaxed at shortstop. He had always been able to throw and run. He was now the complete major-league baseball prospect and was known to professionals who followed baseball throughout the United States.

The 1992 baseball draft took place on June 1, in New York City, and began at 1 P.M. Several scouts had been leaking word to the Jeters that Derek would probably be drafted fifth, by the Cincinnati Reds. Two days before, a man named Dick Groch called the Jeter house. He said he had not called earlier because he did not want to intrude on them. He mentioned that he was a scout for the New York Yankees and that he had been following Derek for two years. He said that his team was very interested in signing Derek but that the Yankees did not pick until the sixth place in the draft. Few expected Derek to still be available that far down.

The sprained ankle may have helped Jeter reach his dream of playing for the Yankees. He was drafted sixth, not first and not fifth, but he was now a New York Yankee. The Jeters were ecstatic. The whole family celebrated. Grandmother Dorothy thought back to that first day with Derek at Yankee Stadium. The dream that started that day had just come true.

Struggling Toward Greatness

The game of baseball was about to become the business of baseball for the Jeter family. The family had always put education first, and they were not about to change. Before the draft, Derek Jeter had been accepted at the University of Michigan, and his family wanted him to go there as soon as baseball allowed. He signed a letter of intent to attend the university and play baseball there. So, by NCAA rules, he could not have a sports agent negotiate a contract with the Yankees. Charles Jeter took over the job and had a crash course in major-league contract negotiations. The one item he insisted on was that the Yankees pay all of Derek's college expenses, whenever and wherever he went to college. After several weeks of tough negotiations, Derek signed his contract on June 28, 1992, for

$800,000, the second-highest amount the Yankees had ever paid for a draft pick at that time. Charles had been a business major before specializing in alcohol and drug counseling, and his business skills helped secure Derek's future.

LEAVING HOME

The sad fact among all the happiness was that the Jeters knew they were about to lose their son, and for good in many ways. He was just now 18 years old and had never left home for an extended period. One of his teachers, Shirley Garzelloni, told a reporter, "If anybody saw that family together, they could understand how hard it must have been to leave them. Derek's so much the big athlete—but there's still some of the little boy in him."

He wanted to spend a week at home after signing with the Yankees so he could be with his family and his girlfriend. He asked if he could at least stay home for the Fourth of July celebration, a holiday he always enjoyed. The Yankees politely told him he needed to report immediately to their minor-league team in Florida. They had made a nearly million-dollar investment and wanted to start to get a return on their investment.

Everyone, especially Sharlee, needed more time. Sharlee was just about to become a teenager, and her big brother had helped her through so much that she knew she was going to be lost without him. Why couldn't he go to college and then play for the Yankees? What would she do without him?

They were all unprepared for what they were feeling as they said goodbye at the Kalamazoo airport. Jeter was fighting back tears. His mother worried in those final moments that he did not know how to cook or iron and was now going to be on his own. His father was quiet, asking only if he was sure he had packed everything. His father later confessed that, as soon as he got back in the car, he broke down and cried uncontrollably.

BAD BEGINNINGS

Jeter flew to Tampa to play in the Gulf Coast Rookie League, his first stop as a professional. Each major-league baseball team operates several minor-league teams. The minor-league system has 19 leagues, and each league has several teams. A Rookie-level team, which primarily has newly signed draftees, is the lowest level. Next up is a Single-A-level team, for young players honing their abilities. A Double-A-level team is for players with more experience who have developed more skill. The Triple-A-level teams have players ready to go to the major leagues, the "Big Show," at a moment's notice. So, players are always on their way up or down in the minor leagues. Everyone has to start there, and no one wants to finish there.

Jeter knew that he would be facing better pitching than he had ever encountered. The best high school pitchers can throw 85 miles per hour (137 kilometers per hour). The slowest professional pitchers throw that fast. Some pitchers at his level might have already had professional experience but might have been returning from an injury. Some were brand new and eager to prove themselves—showing what they could do to get to the next level and not worrying about saving their arms. Jeter also knew that other players would be trying extra hard against him because he had received such a large signing bonus. Word travels fast, and he was a marked man.

After just a few games, Jeter experienced a new sensation. He felt as if he was failing: He was 0-for-14, without a single hit in his first 14 at-bats. He struck out five times in his first seven at-bats. He had not struck out five times in an entire year in high school. The pitches looked as tiny as Tic Tac candies. He felt lost and depressed, wondering if he made the right move in signing with a team right out of high school. Jeter remembers standing on the balcony at the Radisson Bay Harbor Inn in Tampa at the end of the first week, looking out onto the causeway and counting cars. He needed to take his mind off his miserable start as a professional. He missed his family and his home. He missed his friends. He missed everything familiar and was overwhelmed with everything unfamiliar. He even wondered about the University of Michigan and what his roommates would have been like.

When Jeter's hitless streak reached 23 at-bats, a teammate placed a big, red Wiffle-ball bat in his locker, apparently to show Jeter that he should be using a much wider bat or maybe to suggest that he was too young for professional ball. Jeter did not find this funny. He could laugh about it later but not at the time. He felt like an outsider on the team. He had hit the lowest point of his personal and professional life and wondered what could pull him out of this dive. He was failing, he was homesick, and he was sweltering in the soggy Tampa summer. Jeter writes in his autobiography about this miserable time:

> I had doubts. I felt like I was overmatched in everything. The whole game seemed like it was moving in fast-forward. The mound seemed like it was 80 feet away, instead of 60 feet 6 inches. The throw from shortstop to first base felt like I was throwing it from center field to home plate. It seemed like everyone else was on Rollerblades while I was slogging through quicksand. I was using a wooden bat, not aluminum, for the first time, and that was an adjustment. After I made an error in one game, I heard two Spanish-speaking teammates conversing and I figured they were saying, "This is the worst first-round pick I've ever seen."

GETTING HELP

Jeter called his parents and Marisa Novara almost every night, as late as midnight. He received support every time he called. His parents took turns fielding the late calls, each trying to reassure their son that he could succeed, and each trying to keep him from admitting defeat and coming home. Then, they all came to visit within the first month, and again two weeks later. They showed him how much they cared.

The Yankees also helped him. Manager Gary Denbo and minor-league coordinator Mark Newman kept telling him that the Yankees valued him and that he would be a great player some day. Luckily, the Yankees have a rule: They never try to change a player in any way during the first 30 days he is with the organization. They do not want to throw too much at a young player before they are sure what help he needs.

Jeter could have crumbled, but he did not. He had guidance from others around him, and he helped himself by not forgetting what his goals were. He relied on his work ethic. This sense of needing to try harder, which had gotten him through the physical pain in his ankle, helped him through the emotional pain of failure. He relied on his very nature—his competitive personality. He would not let himself be beaten this way. Competitive people can fear their flaws, but Jeter knew his could be corrected.

He never let his self-confidence fall to poisonous levels, and neither did the organization. His coaches explained what he was doing well and what he had not mastered yet. After his six weeks in Tampa, Jeter was batting .202, but he was told that no one would remember what he batted his first year. Even though his first six weeks seemed like six months, he tried to improve by taking two extra weeks with the Yankees' Single-A team in Greensboro, North Carolina, after the Gulf Coast Rookie League season ended.

With his first professional baseball season behind him, Jeter finally headed home to be with his family and friends. He drove his new car, a red Mitsubishi 3000 GT, the one luxury he bought with his bonus money. He also bought his parents a new car, hoping to thank them in some way for all they had done for him. Jeter attended a semester at the University of Michigan in Ann Arbor before returning to baseball the following spring. Jeter loved college. He loved the football games and attended some basketball games. He took some business courses, and he hoped to return to college when his playing days were over. He knew what he was missing by not staying in college, but he was determined to do better in his second year with the Yankees.

1993: TURNING A CORNER

Before reporting to the Greensboro team in 1993, Jeter continued an intense physical and weight-training program he began some months earlier. He had stopped growing at 6-foot-3 but had added several pounds of muscle through hard work in the weight room. Jeter was lucky to have come along in baseball when he did. For most of the previous 50 years, professional baseball teams did not believe in weight training. The common wisdom was that extra muscle would bulk up a player and make it hard for him to have a fluid swing and smooth fielding and running motions. Nothing could be further from the truth.

Jeter knew now what to expect about the game's speed. His reflexes were sharper, and experience enabled him to relax more and react quickly when necessary. In Greensboro, he was surrounded by more experienced players, not just the rookies of the Gulf Coast League. With these more experienced players, he had more teachers and better examples to learn from and follow. Jeter was learning that consistency counted; he needed to be able to do the same things over and over and to realize that one great play did not cancel one terrible play. The terrible play can really hurt the team's ability to win. Jeter was maturing in a very important way.

He had taken the best punch that baseball could throw at him in his first year, and he survived it. His confidence came back, stronger than ever. By the end of the 1993 season, he had hit .295, with 14 doubles, 11 triples (showing his speed), 5 home runs, and 71 runs batted in (RBIs). He also stole 18 bases. His talent and drive had surfaced at the professional level, and he was voted "Most Outstanding Major League Prospect" by the South Atlantic League managers.

Derek Jeter fielded a hit during spring training in 1993 at the Yankees' minor-league complex in Tampa, Florida. In his first season, the year before, Jeter had a jittery time as he got used to his new surroundings. He improved in 1993, batting .295 with the Single-A-level team in Greensboro, North Carolina.

When the 1993 minor-league season ended, Jeter considered returning to college. Instead, he went to the Yankees' complex on North Himes Avenue in Tampa to do extra work on his fielding. He met Brian Butterfield, who looked and acted like a Marine drill sergeant. Butterfield hit him hundreds of ground balls, over and over. He noticed that Jeter was retreating too often when balls were hit to him. He told Jeter to attack the ball when fielding just as he did when hitting. Butterfield analyzed videotapes and showed Jeter how to cut down on wasted motions. Jeter had picked up a bad habit of sliding his glove along the ground when approaching a grounder. One of Jeter's most remarkable characteristics is that he immediately and permanently changes any actions that are hurting his play, once they are pointed out to him. He does not change slowly or eventually. He changes quickly and for good. The hours of drilling gave Jeter backaches and leg pain, but the effort paid off. He was eliminating errors and becoming consistent, treating each ground ball the same way. His extra work at the complex made him ready to excel in 1994.

1994 AND THE STRIKE

The third year started out to be the charm for Jeter. He was sent again to Tampa, this time to the Yankees' highest Single-A-level team, not the Rookie league squad. He did so well there that he was soon promoted to the Yankees' Double-A team in Albany, New York. The higher he went, the better he did. He was quickly promoted again, this time to the best minor-league team in the Yankees' system, the Triple-A Columbus Clippers. He hit a whopping .349 in 35 games for the Clippers and fielded well. Everyone in the organization knew that he would soon be with the big-league team. Yankee Stadium was so close he could feel it.

Baseball fans know what happened in 1994. The major-league players and owners could not agree on salary and other issues, and the players walked out in the middle of August. The World Series was canceled. Generations of fan interest had

After being named the "Minor League Player of the Year" for 1994 by *Baseball America*, Derek Jeter posed with the trophy on the dugout steps at Yankee Stadium. During the season, he moved up from Single-A ball to the Triple-A team in Columbus, Ohio. If not for the major-league baseball strike late in the season, Jeter might have made it to "The Show" in 1994.

evaporated. People were disgusted with the owners and the players, and a certain number of fans have not returned to the game, even to this day.

The strike delayed Jeter's grand entrance into Yankee Stadium, but it might have actually helped him. He had to stay longer at Columbus, and that may have further refined his skills. New Yorkers were so desperate for baseball that a Clippers game was actually televised in the Yankees' market, and people got their first look at this up-and-coming shortstop. Perhaps this exposure helped him win *Baseball America's* "Minor League Player of the Year" award. He earned similar awards from the *Sporting News* and *Baseball Weekly.* With no major-league news to report, the minor-league players received more attention and became better known.

EARLY 1995: THE TIME IS NOW

While baseball officials were trying to reach an agreement to end the strike before the 1995 season started, players worked out at their normal spring-training camps. The Yankees' camp had been at Fort Lauderdale Stadium in Florida for 34 years, and 1995 would be the final season there. The stadium was getting old, and the blue seats were worn. The fans were so close to the players that they all could talk in a normal voice and hear one another clearly. As it happened, Yankees great Don Mattingly was coming into his final year before retirement. He was a legend with Yankee fans and had been with the team his entire career, but he had never won a World Series. One day during spring training, Mattingly taught Jeter a memorable lesson. Jeter describes what happened:

> I finished my wind sprints the same time as Mattingly that day. We were both sweating and exhaling as we scooped up our gloves and started back to the clubhouse. . . . There were no players or coaches on the field, and the fans had bolted.

I've been in churches that were noisier. But Mattingly did not let the emptiness change what he was about.

"Let's run in," Mattingly told me. "You never know who is watching."

So we ran. Side by side, stride for stride, across the green grass of the outfield, to the dirt of the infield, past the grass around the pitcher's mound.... Our spikes clicked across the asphalt path as we finally stopped running. It took us about 30 seconds, but that brief experience meant a lot to me.... There's a saying that the true character of a man is revealed by what he does when no one is watching. So, even if the stadium looked empty and even if Steinbrenner [the Yankee owner] wasn't in Florida, Mattingly did what was proper.

THE STRIKE

On August 12, 1994, professional baseball players went on strike. The walkout was the eighth work stoppage in baseball's history and the third in 23 years to occur during the playing season. The strike lasted 232 days; 938 games were canceled, including the 1994 World Series. Baseball became the first sport in history to lose its postseason. Some estimate that $1 billion was lost by players and team owners, the two sides in the battle. When it ended, neither side had given in. The only change was that hundreds of thousands of fans had lost interest in the game. Two world wars, the Great Depression, and earthquakes had never stopped the World Series. Greed and selfishness did.

The main issue, of course, was money. The players wanted to make as much as they could, and the owners wanted to put

The strike ended in April 1995, and Jeter started the season where he left off the year before, in Columbus. The Yankees had seen his hard work in spring training, and everyone knew he was heading up to the Yankees soon. On May 28, the Jeter family got the call they had been hoping for. Sharlee answered the phone and heard her brother's excitement. She handed the phone to her father, who heard his son say, "I'm going to the big leagues." Jeter explained that the regular Yankee shortstop, Tony Fernández, was slightly injured and that Jeter had to get to Seattle to join the team. Charles immediately booked a flight to Seattle. Dorothy stayed with Sharlee, who had a softball game that night. As they always had, each parent was going to a game for one of the children.

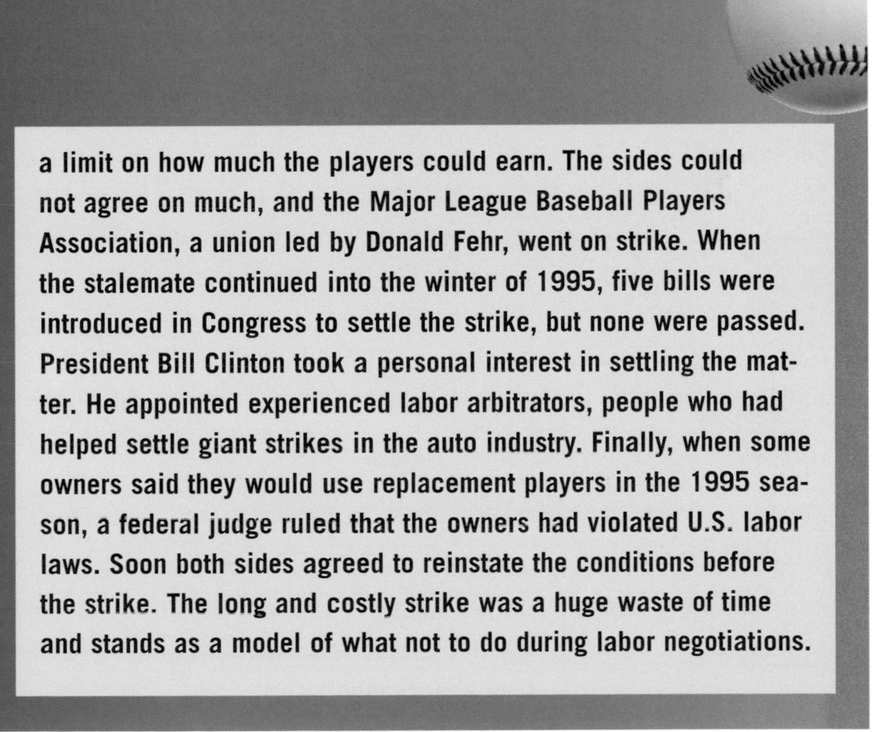

a limit on how much the players could earn. The sides could not agree on much, and the Major League Baseball Players Association, a union led by Donald Fehr, went on strike. When the stalemate continued into the winter of 1995, five bills were introduced in Congress to settle the strike, but none were passed. President Bill Clinton took a personal interest in settling the matter. He appointed experienced labor arbitrators, people who had helped settle giant strikes in the auto industry. Finally, when some owners said they would use replacement players in the 1995 season, a federal judge ruled that the owners had violated U.S. labor laws. Soon both sides agreed to reinstate the conditions before the strike. The long and costly strike was a huge waste of time and stands as a model of what not to do during labor negotiations.

Before a game at Yankee Stadium in 1995, Derek Jeter waited to take batting practice. Jeter was called up to the Yankees for a few weeks in May and June of 1995 and again in September. He played in 15 games altogether in the major leagues that season.

Jeter went hitless in five at-bats on his first night. He and his father went to McDonald's after the game. The next night, Jeter got a hit off Mariners pitcher Tim Belcher, and his father leapt out of his seat. Some fans must have wondered why the man was so excited when a Yankee unknown got a hit. They would soon know this unknown player.

DOWN AND UP

Jeter was overjoyed to be with the team and wanted to fit in. He also knew that he was still learning. During a rain delay, Mattingly, his new friend and mentor, offered some advice. Mattingly noticed that Jeter hesitated before he threw the ball to first base from shortstop, and he joked that Jeter was giving him, the first baseman, heart failure. This was the big leagues, and players were quicker to get to first base. There was little time or reason to delay the throw. He suggested that Jeter develop a more fluid motion from catching the ball to throwing, much as Orioles shortstop Cal Ripken, Jr., did. Jeter reacted in his typical way. He listened carefully and started to practice as soon as he got back to his hotel room. He stood in front of a full-length mirror and changed the way he had done something for a dozen years. He learned, did not take the advice as criticism, and made his game better.

Jeter tried not to think about what would happen when Tony Fernández's rib injury healed. He wanted to stay in the big leagues. On June 11, the Yankees beat Seattle, 10-7, at Yankee Stadium, and the team was about to get on a plane to Detroit for a series with the Tigers. A group of nearly 100 of Jeter's fans from Kalamazoo was making the drive to Tiger Stadium for a homecoming of sorts. Everyone was excited to see the hometown hero. Jeter was called into manager Buck Showalter's office just before leaving, and he was told he was going back to Columbus since Fernández was able to play again. Some part of Jeter must have known this move was coming, but he was hoping against hope. He was devastated. It would be several moments before he could make another call to his parents, this time with bad news. Mattingly pulled him aside and said, "You will be back." He said it in such a way that Jeter believed him.

Mattingly was right. In September, teams are able to add more players to their rosters. Jeter was called up and waited for his chance. It came on September 26. One of the Yankees, Bernie Williams, had returned to Puerto Rico to see his newborn daughter and had missed his flight to Milwaukee, where the Yankees were playing the Brewers in an important game. The Yankees were only one game ahead in the wild-card race to get into the postseason. They needed to win. In the second inning, in his first important and pressure-filled at-bat in the major leagues, Jeter hit a rocket to left-center field, good for a double. He then scored the first run of the game. He always remembered that at-bat, and he used it to motivate him to run harder and lift more weights.

The Yankees made it into the postseason but lost in the first round, the American League Division Series, to the Seattle Mariners. It was a disappointment, but Jeter had shown what he could do in pressure situations. Managers remember that. He had a good feeling as he headed into the fateful 1996 season.

Living the Dream

Spring training for the Yankees in 1996 began on February 20, at a new complex, Legends Field, in Tampa. The Yankees also had a new manager, Joe Torre, who called a team meeting and told everyone that he expected this team to go to the World Series. He said that every one of the team's coaches had been to the World Series except him, and he planned to change that. He was met with silence and stares. No Yankee team had been to the World Series in 15 years or won one in 18 years, and the clubhouse had been a revolving door of players and managers. Yankees owner George Steinbrenner had lost patience with many managers, and few expected Torre to last. He had a losing record as a manager for other teams. If the past was a prediction for the future, the future did not look good. Don Mattingly, the Yankee captain and best player, had retired. The team did not have a proven shortstop. Not many sportswriters had high hopes for the Yankees that year. And the fans had fewer hopes.

THE NEW YANKEES

Some good signs, however, did exist. The Yankees under Steinbrenner had been famous for trading away minor leaguers with potential for experienced players who were expensive but proven. Gradually, as the failures of that strategy became more obvious, the Yankees changed their ways. They started to develop their minor leaguers and give them a chance to prove themselves. Some of those players were now ready for the big leagues. Center fielder Bernie Williams, pitcher Andy Pettitte, and another pitcher who had been with Jeter on several minor-league teams, Mariano Rivera, were all now in the majors together.

Outfielder Paul O'Neill had developed into a strong player whose intensity was obvious to all. Pitcher David Cone was a proven winner. Tino Martinez, a solid first baseman, had been added to the team. Yankees fans would later realize that a rare set of conditions had brought together so many young players on the same team at the same time. No one could know that Rivera would develop into one of the best relief pitchers of all time, that Bernie Williams would become a brilliant center fielder and hitter, and that Pettitte would become a great pitcher as well. O'Neill and Jim Leyritz would become clutch players. The Yankees were poised to be great, but no one knew it in the spring of 1996.

In many ways, the biggest question mark was at shortstop. The Yankees still had Tony Fernández, but they also liked what they saw of Jeter in 1995. When spring training got under way, and Torre got a better and longer look at Jeter, it became clear that the 21-year-old rookie would get his chance. Jeter may have struggled at the plate, but Torre had heard that the more

Derek Jeter, throwing to first base to complete the double play, jumped over the Mariners' Rich Amaral after forcing him out at second base during a 1996 game in Yankee Stadium. Before the season began, some in the Yankees organization had doubts that Jeter could be their long-term shortstop.

important the situation, the better Jeter seemed to play. Jeter never did well in spring training, when the stakes were low. Increasing expectations from others made Jeter want to meet and exceed them.

Baseball has nine players on the field at a time, and no position except pitcher is more important defensively than the shortstop. This fielder must cover a great deal of ground, and since more hitters are right-handed, more balls are hit to the shortstop's side of the field (the left side of the infield). To start a season with a new shortstop, a rookie shortstop, never inspires a great deal of confidence in a team. Too much is unknown. Five different shortstops had started for the Yankees in the past five years, and no one believed that the team's search had ended when Torre penciled in the name of Derek Jeter on the lineup card to start the 1996 season. It is thought that Steinbrenner came into Torre's office a week before the season started and asked if they should trade for a veteran shortstop, someone they knew could at least hold down the position for another year. Jeter had not done well during spring training, and people within the organization were having doubts. Torre apparently told Steinbrenner that it was too late to change, and, with luck, Jeter could hit .250 and not embarrass the team.

The team had given Jeter the number 2. Besides No. 6, it was the only single-digit number that the Yankees had not retired. Jeter had never had this number before; at Kalamazoo he was No. 13, but that was already taken. Most baseball players are superstitious, but Jeter must have enjoyed No. 13. He would go on to enjoy his new number as well. Later, at the end of the year, he would laugh when he saw the parade signs that said, "No. 2 is No. 1."

THE BEGINNING OF A CHAMPIONSHIP SEASON

The Yankees' 1996 season began on April 2, in Cleveland. On Opening Day, 42,289 fans were at Jacobs Field; one of them was Dorothy Jeter. Her son had always looked for his parents before a game. It seemed to calm him down when he found them in their seats. That day, he searched for his mother but had trouble finding her. More fans were at this game than he was used to seeing. He knew that his father was watching Sharlee play a softball game at Kalamazoo Central and that his mother was there at Jacobs Field somewhere. That was enough.

Jeter went to Torre just before the game and tried to reassure him. The shortstop knew that his manager was in his first game with the Yankees as well, and Jeter wanted him to know that they would get through this season together. The two had already developed a bond of trust and respect. That bond would grow stronger by the day. Jeter then went out and hit a home run off Dennis Martínez and made a spectacular catch over his shoulder, perhaps the most difficult play a shortstop is asked to make. The Yankees won, 7-1. Looking back, Torre remembered the day clearly when he spoke to reporters:

> I received two pleasant surprises on Opening Day: a huge good-luck basket of goodies from my friend Big Julie Isaacson and a stunning performance by Jeter. . . . Once the season started, it was as if he jumped into a phone booth and changed into a Superman costume. The rookie made a great catch of a pop fly and hit a home run—signs of things to come.

A few days later, the Yankees had their home opener. In the turf-covered runway that goes from their clubhouse to their first-base dugout, a blue metal sign hangs from the ceiling. It says, "I want to thank the Good Lord for making me a Yankee." Joe DiMaggio spoke those words on October 1, 1949. Jeter always passes under the sign and touches it with his hand or glove, a ritual he started that first day at Yankee Stadium. He does it because he is superstitious but also because he agrees with DiMaggio. In his autobiography, he explains some of what he sees and feels as he takes the field:

> I love digging my spikes into the brown clay; I love how the light frames the field, and I even love the smell of hot dogs and hot pretzels that wafts down on us. Then there are the creative fans, who are the loudest I've ever heard and who make us feel special during every game. . . . Most of my life was spent working toward that elusive goal of becoming a major leaguer and most of my life now is spent on keeping me here at a high level. My goal is simple: to keep getting better. . . . I like to chase my dreams, and I advise everyone else to do the same.

When the team played its first home game on April 9, Jeter had one hit and scored a run. For the first time, he heard the roar of the home crowd celebrating a hit. Over the next few months, that roar would start when he came to bat. In the middle of May, the team was comfortably in first place in the American League East. Jeter was hitting the ball and making plays. He was fast enough to beat out infield hits one after another, forcing opposing infielders to rush their throws to try to get him out. He just may be the fastest right-handed hitter in the league, getting to first base as quickly as any player in recent history. Casual fans who did not know much about Jeter were amazed that he was doing so well as a 21-year-old rookie.

A LEADER THROUGH A LONG SEASON

The team's fast start did not last. One of the Yankees' best pitchers, David Cone, developed an aneurysm in his pitching arm. An aneurysm results when weakness in a vein or an artery allows blood to push out the vein or artery wall and collect in a kind of pocket. If the aneurysm bursts, it can be fatal. When his teammates heard that Cone needed an operation to save his life, they were stunned. He might never play again. Several experts felt that the season was now over for this young team. By August, the Yankees' early 10-game lead had almost vanished.

Jeter had a 17-game hitting streak, the longest streak by a Yankees rookie since Joe DiMaggio's 60 years earlier, and he helped keep the team together during its slump. Jeter had bad days of his own, though. During one game in Chicago, the score was tied in the eighth inning. One of the Yankee power hitters, Cecil Fielder, came to the plate with two outs with Jeter on first base. Jeter tried to steal second base and was thrown out. Torre was furious. When a player makes such a serious mistake, he usually returns to the dugout and sits as far from the manager as he can, to avoid a confrontation. Hiding is not Jeter's style. He came in, sat right next to Torre, and heard a stream of angry words about not stealing unless he got a sign. Jeter took the heat, remained calm, and learned.

In his first season, Jeter did something that drove all of his coaches a little crazy. Before an at-bat, he liked to talk to kids beside the Yankees' dugout. He would ask them if he should bunt or swing at the first pitch or try to hit to right field. They answered him, and gave him advice and encouragement. If a kid asked a question, Jeter would try to answer it. Yankee coaches did not ever remember a player doing this, and they gently tried to break him of the habit. To this day, however, Jeter continues to talk to his fans during the game.

He can somehow flip a mental switch and begin to concentrate fully as soon as he steps into the batter's box. And even before then. From the on-deck circle, Jeter will watch the pitcher and try to determine if he is throwing fastballs on the first pitch or see if his slider is breaking sharply. He knows he can hit pitches just above his shoes or way outside. Pitchers try to keep hitters guessing. Jeter reverses that. He keeps pitchers guessing about which pitches he will swing at.

His coaches learned to adjust to his habits, since he was proving to be a team leader. He seemed to be an emotional leader who could keep his teammates from fighting with one another as well as a tension reliever who could prevent the team from getting too tight. Jeter describes his leadership style:

Derek Jeter signed autographs before a game against the Red Sox in 1997. Before an at-bat, Jeter will often talk to kids sitting beside the Yankees' dugout. He answers their questions and takes their advice and encouragement. His coaches tried to break him of the habit, but they could not.

I think I'm a mixture of leading by example and leading by tweaking guys. . . . I'm always enthused and always confident. . . . That's my personality. I'll never change and I hope it calms others down and helps our team. You can do a lot for friends and colleagues by always being positive and optimistic. . . . We spend seven months together, so there's got to be camaraderie that goes beyond baseball. I think I know when to push the right buttons with different players because I watch my teammates and know how far the guys will let you go. I'm always playful, never too personal.

Jeter's leadership, together with David Cone's return on Labor Day and a productive September from several players, propelled the Yankees to win the American League East Division on September 25. Jeter hit .314 for the season, with 10 home runs and 78 runs batted in. He would later be named the 1996 American League Rookie of the Year. The season, though, was not over.

THE 1996 POSTSEASON: CHAMPIONS!

The Yankees played the hard-hitting Texas Rangers in the first round of the 1996 playoffs. During his first game in the playoffs, Jeter had an off night and made a key out with the bases loaded in the sixth inning. The Yankees lost the game, 6-2. As is typical, Jeter did not let his performance bother him, and he went on to score the winning run in the twelfth inning the next night. That 5-4 victory seemed to deflate the Rangers. The Yankees won the next two games and advanced to the American League Championship Series against the Baltimore Orioles. The two teams had been bitter rivals over the years, and many fans were looking forward to this matchup.

Game 1 of the 1996 American League Championship Series was close and exciting. In the eighth inning at Yankee Stadium, Jeter hit one of the most famous home runs in baseball history. The Yankees were losing, 4-3, when Jeter came to the plate. He hit a long fly to right field off pitcher Armando Benítez, and a 12-year-old boy in the stands leaned out and caught the ball just before the leaping Oriole right fielder could get it in his glove. The umpire ruled the hit a home run, and the boy, Jeffrey Maier, became a hero or a villain, depending on which side you were on. Writer Patrick Giles describes the moment in his biography of Jeter:

> There *was* something magical about that moment. The adult Jeter hit the ball, it almost sailed out of the park, and it got

On a ball hit by Derek Jeter in Game 1 of the 1996 American League Championship Series, Baltimore Orioles right fielder Tony Tarasco stretched to make the catch. But the ball was deflected into the stands by young Yankees fan Jeffrey Maier. Jeter's hit was ruled a home run, tying the game at 4-4. The Yankees went on to win the game, and the play has become legendary.

caught by a boy like Jeter once was, a boy who loved baseball and whose ready hand and glove changed the history of the Series. If you look quickly at the video of that moment, you can almost imagine the boy Jeter catching the ball sent to him by Jeter the man.

The Yankees went on to win the game and the series against the Orioles. Most fans described the home run by Jeter as the pivotal point.

The Atlanta Braves were the heavy favorite to win the 1996 World Series. They were the defending champions, and had pitching, power, youth, and experience. Very few experts thought that the Yankees had a chance. The experts were wrong. Even though the Braves won the first two games at Yankee Stadium, the Yankees came back to sweep the next four games and win the World Championship. Every starting player contributed either a key hit or a spectacular fielding play. Starting pitchers Cone and Pettitte had big wins. Relief pitchers Mariano Rivera and John Wetteland held the Braves down in the late innings. The team had come together in a way that few teams ever did. By the end of the third game, they were unstoppable. Everyone could feel it.

Joe Torre would later say that, every time the Yankees needed a rally, Jeter seemed to start one. Jeter was hit on the wrist by a fastball from Greg Maddux in Game 2, but he fought through the injury just as he had done in the cold days of April several years before with his ankle. In the locker room after the final victory, Jeter was surrounded by reporters, soaked in champagne, blinded by the camera lights, saying, "I'm just so happy. It's just magic."

THE POSTSEASON FRENZY: A CELEBRITY'S LIFE

Jeter was the youngest player on the World Champions. He was good-looking, polite, articulate, smart, and now a media darling. Suddenly, it seemed that every newspaper and magazine in America wanted to profile this emerging superstar, even the *New York Times*. The *Times* put Jeter on the cover of its *Men's Fashions of the Times* magazine in March 1997. Everyone agreed—Jeter seemed to project confidence and success. He describes that confidence:

You should always think that you're going to be successful, and you should always want to be successful. If it doesn't work out for you and you strike out with the winning run on third or you fail your driver's test, you have to acknowledge that something went wrong, and adjust your actions and go

JEFFREY MAIER

He is famous as the 12-year-old boy from Old Tappan, New Jersey, who "gave" Derek Jeter a home run and sent the 1996 Yankees on their way to the American League Championship and to a World Championship. On October 9, 1996, during the first game of the American League Championship Series, the Yankees were trailing the Baltimore Orioles, 4-3, in the eighth inning. Up at bat was the Yankees' sensational rookie shortstop. This at-bat was probably the biggest of his career up to that point. Jeter connected on a long fly ball to right center field, and Orioles right fielder Tony Tarasco raced back to the wall. He jumped as high as he could to catch the ball but was astonished that the ball never came down into his glove. Someone else had caught the ball, or at least deflected it into the stands. Tarasco looked up to see Jeffrey Maier, who had reached out over the wall with perfect timing. The ball hit the heel of Jeffrey's glove and bounced up to his chest and down to the floor.

Right-field umpire Rich Garcia immediately and decisively raised his right arm and made a circle in the air, signaling a home run. Later, after seeing a replay, he would admit that the hit was not a home run because Jeffrey had reached into the field of play and interfered with the ball. He should have ruled fan interference, and no home run.

after it again the next time. The next time you try that task, don't think about the time you faltered. Think about all of the times in which you have excelled. . . . You've got to find that confidence, even if it's only a sliver of confidence on some days, and cling to it.

Some people said that Jeffrey was Jeter's "angel in the outfield." Others were cruel, saying that the boy had reached the high point of his life at 12. He was called a hero, a punk, and a truant (he had skipped school that day). Some people loved him, and some hated him. Some fans said he should be punished, and others said he should be rewarded. He became a celebrity briefly, even appearing on the *Late Show with David Letterman*.

Maier went on to star in baseball at Wesleyan University in Connecticut. In April 2006, he set the all-time school record for hits. He has had to endure Red Sox and Oriole fans yelling at him and throwing snow and ice balls at him during his college games. He even had to endure a fellow Wesleyan student making a movie called *I Hate Jeffrey Maier*. He is philosophical about it all; he explained to *Boston Globe* reporter Stan Grossfield: "You live life without regrets. Everything happens for a reason. I haven't quite figured out what the reason is yet, but I don't have any regrets about it." He cherishes the ball that Jeter signed and gave him after the season was over. It reads, "To Jeff. Thanks a lot, Derek Jeter." Since Jeffrey was almost trampled by older people who took the "home run" ball away from him, the signed Jeter ball is even more special. He will not be putting it on eBay anytime soon.

Jeter was the toast of New York City and was soon invited to many parties and celebrations. He went to a Fresh Air Fund benefit in November 1996 and met someone who changed his life. Mariah Carey was four years older and already a pop-singing phenomenon. She, too, had an Irish-American mother and an African-American father and had never met anyone else with the same heritage. Her parents were married in 1960, four years before the landmark Civil Rights Act, and they had to endure even more discrimination than Jeter's parents. (Her parents had their dog poisoned and their car set on fire by people trying to scare them out of predominantly white neighborhoods). By all accounts, she and Jeter became fast friends almost immediately. They enjoyed each other's company, partly because of what they had in common and partly because both were so successful. Carey was married at the time to Tommy Mottola, a powerful music industry executive, and people disagree on whether a real romance between the two stars developed then. There is no doubt that they eventually became close.

Derek Jeter was no longer just an athlete. He was a full-fledged celebrity, with all the attention and coverage that entails. He was stalked by photographers, inundated with love letters, besieged by interview requests. He became, like all celebrities, a fantasy figure. Media companies create and nurture these fantasy figures because it is profitable for them. Some athletes cannot stand the pressure that comes with this elevation in attention. Remarkably, Jeter could. All players get nervous before big games, but they learn to turn nervousness into excitement, not fear. Jeter is one of the few who resisted pressures off the field as well. He kept his equilibrium. He has not trashed a hotel room, been arrested for drunken driving, or changed in any public way. He may be paying a price that only he and his family can see, but his character and upbringing have prepared him for whatever the celebrity industry can throw at him. Jeter has said that his number-one priority has been to do well at baseball, and that priority has not changed.

1997: A LETDOWN

The 1997 New York Yankees are a team that fans pay little attention to now, because the dramatic World Series victory in 1996 and the superlative 1998 season overshadow the year in between. Many people assume that the 1997 Yankees were just not as good a team as either the 1996 or 1998 squads. The statistics tell a different story. The 1997 Yankees won more games, scored 20 more runs, and allowed a whopping 99 fewer runs than the 1996 team. They finished second to the Baltimore Orioles not because they were inferior to the 1996 team, but because the Orioles had gotten better during 1997. The Orioles lost to the Cleveland Indians in the American League Championship Series, and a disappointing season closed for them. (The Yankees had lost to the Indians in the Division Series.)

Jeter did not do as well in 1997 as he had in 1996, another reason that the 1997 Yankees are a forgotten team. His batting average dropped from .314 to .291. His strikeouts rose from 102 to 125. He had worked specifically on trying to strike out less during the 1997 season, and he had failed. Some in the Yankees organization worried that he might have been a one-year wonder, a flash in the pan. Some felt that the search for a long-term shortstop was not over and that all the attention Jeter received was distracting him from the game.

The 1997 World Series pitted the Cleveland Indians against the Florida Marlins. Jeter went to the second game in Miami but found that he could not stay past the first few innings. Being there hurt too much. He knew his team was good, and he hated the thought that it should have been the Yankees and not the Indians playing for the championship. He vowed that he would never have that feeling again:

A dejected Derek Jeter looked out from the dugout on October 6, 1997, after the Cleveland Indians won the American League Division Series, eliminating the Yankees from the postseason. Jeter's 1997 season was a bit of a disappointment, too, after his stellar rookie year.

Have you ever felt that someone picked the wrong student to play the lead in the play or the wrong person for that sweet summer job? It should have been you, right? While I moped about our loss for a few months, I didn't let the loss turn me into a couch potato. You can't let those setbacks ruin your enthusiasm. I went into 1998 fresh and ready.

Players often talk about how winning in New York City is expected and how bitter losing there is. Every play, every inning, every game is magnified, for better or worse. As high as the team was after the unexpected 1996 season, there was a corresponding low after 1997. It was a low that did not last long.

On Top of the World

Fans who came to the Yankees' spring-training camp in 1998 were treated to several sightings of Mariah Carey. The relationship between Jeter and Carey had strengthened, and Carey had obtained a divorce from Tommy Mottola. The couple were seen all over Tampa that spring, and the attention never stopped. Reporters from throughout the world came to Legends Field to interview Jeter—not about baseball but about his love life.

1998 REGULAR SEASON: THE BEST TEAM EVER?

If the Yankees thought that all of this attention would hurt Jeter, they did not need to worry. Jeter and the Yankees got off to a fast start, and by the end of May, the team was 37–13, 7½ games ahead of the Boston Red Sox in the American

League East. David Wells pitched a perfect game against the Minnesota Twins on May 17, and David Cone also continued his strong pitching. He would go on to win 20 games. Each player seemed intent on doing his job, whether to score runs or prevent the other team from scoring. Jeter was more than doing his part. He continued to improve and to do even the small tasks well—he moved runners from first to second or second to third by deliberately hitting to the right side. He bunted when he had to, stole a base when it mattered, made the extra effort not to let a ball get through the left side of the infield.

The Yankees went on to win 114 games during the regular season, losing only 48, the second-best winning percentage in major-league history. They hit 207 home runs, the second-most in Yankee history. Eight Yankees hit more than 15 homers. The team was filled with unselfish players who rooted for one another, worked extremely hard at improving their hitting and fielding, and never took their eyes off the prize of getting to the postseason. Many consider the 1998 Yankees among the best teams in the history of baseball.

Jeter was elected to play in the 1998 All-Star Game, his first appearance. By the end of the season, he had hit a personal-best .324 and had 30 stolen bases. Some mentioned him as a contender to win the American League Most Valuable Player award, one of the highest honors in professional baseball. As always, he reacted to questions about his personal accomplishments the way he might if someone were feeding him cod liver oil. He hated to dwell on what he had done but enjoyed celebrating what others had accomplished.

He had hit 19 homers by the 143rd game of the season and changed his swing to try to hit No. 20. He wanted that milestone, after hitting only 10 home runs in each of his first two years. The change in his swing proved to be a mistake, since he never did hit his twentieth. His batting average dropped

10 points in the final weeks, taking him out of the running for the league's highest honor.

As always, he learned a lesson. He never again tried to be something he was not. Jeter was not a natural home-run hitter and never had been. He had always just tried to hit the ball hard, not hit upward so it would carry farther. Balls fly farther if they have backspin on them, and a swing designed to put more backspin on the ball would be a new swing for Jeter. He liked to hit to the opposite field if the pitch was not on the inside part of home plate, and he once hit an opposite-field home run to the upper deck without trying. When he tried to hit home runs, he found he made too many changes to his swing and was more off-balance. So, he stayed with the swing that had served him well since Little League.

The 1998 season was a wonderful one for all of baseball. Mark McGwire and Sammy Sosa battled all year to see who could break the single-season home-run record (61) of Yankee great Roger Maris. McGwire ended the season with 70 home runs, and Sosa had 66. The 1994 strike was not forgotten, but many fans came back to the game to watch the home-run derby and to see the great Yankees team. As they headed into the playoffs, it seemed as if nothing could stop the team from New York.

1998 POSTSEASON: AN UNSTOPPABLE FORCE

The Texas Rangers were supposed to be able to hit any pitching. In the first round of the 1998 playoffs against the Yankees, they managed one run in three games. The Yankees advanced easily to the American League Championship Series against the Cleveland Indians, the same team that had knocked the Yankees out of the postseason the year before. The Indians seemed unafraid of these Yankees, offering up a tough battle.

In the first game of the championship series at Yankee Stadium, Indian Travis Fryman hit a sharp ground ball to deep

Derek Jeter made a spectacular play on a ground ball hit by Travis Fryman in the first game of the 1998 American League Championship Series against the Cleveland Indians. He lunged to his right, backhanded the ball, and threw it in midair to first base to get Fryman out.

shortstop. It was almost certainly a hit that could start the rally the Indians needed. Jeter sprang to his right, backhanded the ball, and in midair, threw to first to get Fryman. Fans looked at one another in amazement. How did he do that? They roared their approval and gave Jeter a standing ovation. The Indians' rally never happened, and the Yankees went on to win that game, 7-2.

The Indians won the next two games, however, and suddenly the glorious 1998 season seemed in jeopardy. Yankee batters went into a mini-slump in Games 2, 3, and 4, but the Yankee pitchers, led by Orlando Hernández (nicknamed "El Duque"), came to the rescue. Hernández shut out the Indians in the crucial Game 4, and the Indians did not win another game. The turning point in the final game, Game 6, was a triple by Jeter that knocked in two runs. The Yankees were headed to their second World Series in three years.

Yankee Stadium on a late-October evening for a World Series opening game is a very special place. Some of the richest and most famous people in one of the richest and most famous cities gather to see and be seen. In 1998, Jack Nicholson, Bruce Willis, Barbara Walters, and Sarah Michelle Gellar were just four of the prominent fans. Jeter told reporters that the World Series at Yankee Stadium is "like a Broadway play; it's center stage. The World Series should be played in New York. Hopefully, it will be played here for awhile. It's fun; it's the pinnacle of sports."

Perhaps visiting the pinnacle was a bit too much for the San Diego Padres, winners of the National League pennant. This would be the thirty-fifth World Series for the Yankees, and only the second for the Padres. Led by a grand slam by Tino Martinez in the seventh inning, the Yankees won the first game, 9-6. Orlando Hernández beat the Padres in Game 2, 9-3. Scott Brosius was the Yankees' hero in Game 3, hitting two home runs, and Andy Pettitte and Bernie Williams took their

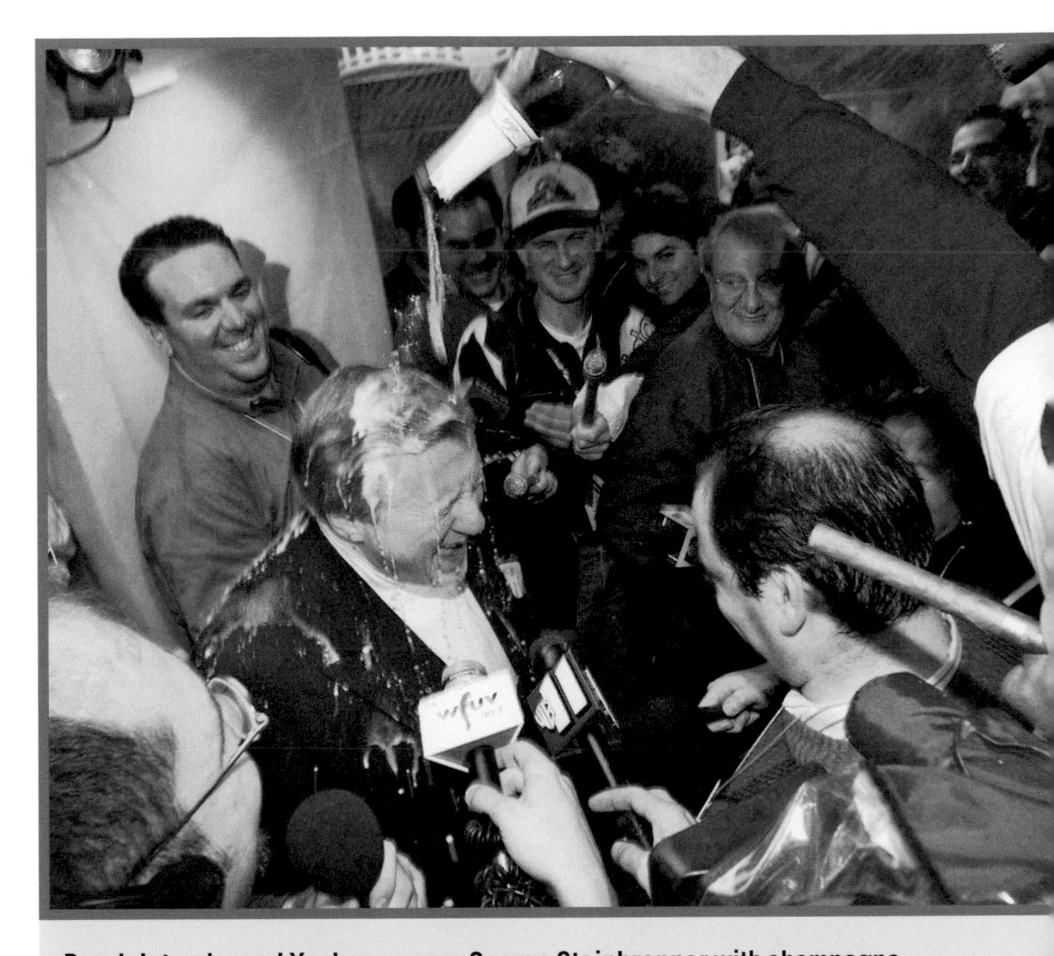

Derek Jeter doused Yankees owner George Steinbrenner with champagne after New York beat Cleveland in the American League Championship Series on October 13, 1998. Steinbrenner got a similar soaking a short time later, when the Yankees swept the San Diego Padres to win the World Series.

turns as heroes in the finale, Game 4. The Yankees swept the Padres and were once again world champions.

In the visitors' clubhouse at Qualcomm Stadium in San Diego, the Yankees celebrated after the fourth game. Jeter took a bottle of 1989 Perrier-Jouet Brut champagne and splashed owner George Steinbrenner's blue blazer, white turtleneck, and groomed hair—just as he had bathed the Boss a few games earlier after the championship series. Very few people would have had the nerve to douse the Yankees' owner, but Jeter was both fearless and ecstatic. The owner laughed as hard as he ever had.

Counting the postseason, the 1998 Yankees won 125 games while only losing 50, a major-league record for most wins in an entire season. They had played well in every phase of the game for a whole season. They could hit home runs, and they could run out ground balls. They showed respect for other teams and were not loud and boastful. They were smart. Even Yankee haters had to admire them. They joined the other great teams in baseball: the 1927 Yankees, with Babe Ruth and Lou Gehrig; the 1961 Yankees, with Mickey Mantle, Roger Maris, Whitey Ford, and Yogi Berra; and the 1976 Cincinnati Reds, with Joe Morgan, Pete Rose, Johnny Bench, and Tony Pérez. They were a team for the ages.

OUT ON THE TOWN

Jetermania became even more intense after the second championship in 1998. People pointed at Jeter when he walked around New York, whispering and nodding in a way they did not do with most celebrities. Jeter's personal life became more noteworthy. His day-to-day habits were the subject of endless reports. Fans found out that he watched ESPN and liked Michael Jordan, Pete Sampras, and Jennifer Capriati. He followed University of Michigan football and basketball. His favorite actors were Samuel L. Jackson and Morgan Freeman. His favorite color was blue (but not Dodger blue).

His eating habits became more famous as well. He enjoyed spaghetti and meatballs, and chicken parmigiana. He loved Frosted Flakes. Fans now knew that he liked Caesar salads with grilled chicken and iced tea at Brunell's on York Avenue. At Veruka in New York's SoHo district, Jeter and his friends received more attention than movie actors. The owner of the

China Club, a favorite Jeter hangout, was constantly asked when Jeter was coming in. Moomba and Jimmy's Bronx Café grew in popularity as Yankee sightings increased.

One of Jeter's closest friends, David Cone, said that going out with Jeter was like going out with Elvis Presley. Tim Raines, another teammate, noted that women flocked to Jeter when he went out with friends in New York. Jeter has always liked going out in groups, where companions can be with him but also provide a natural barrier to onlookers. When he was in the minor leagues, he invited his entire team to go to the movies or to a restaurant. He liked smaller groups now and enjoyed going out to clubs and restaurants with Cone, Raines, Tino Martinez, Jorge Posada, and Jim Leyritz. He looked out for his friends, and they looked out for him.

Jeter has a way of handling all the attention. He stays in control, and his body language lets people know he is friendly but also careful. He seems to have time for his fans, but virtually all of them know they should not push too hard to get a picture or an autograph. Only rarely did Jeter get the sense he was being followed by a fan trying to get too familiar.

Jeter's celebrity, and his abilities, made him a good deal of money. After the 1998 season, he went to arbitration, a process of resolving salary disputes. The Yankees offered him $3.2 million for the 1999 season, but Jeter felt he deserved more. He had taken enough business courses and had enough advice from his father to know his worth. A panel of independent experts during arbitration agreed with him, awarding him a salary of $5 million for the next season.

Rather than letting that much money go to his head, he used it to motivate himself. Instead of making him contented or lazy, the money seemed to make him even hungrier. For every hour he spent in a restaurant or a club, he spent many more hours weight training at the Yankees' complex in Tampa or the International Performance Institute in Bradenton, Florida. Each off-season he worked to strengthen his legs, arms, and mid-body. He lifted weights and worked with a physioball, which is like a heavy medicine ball. Unlike several other major-league stars, Jeter has never been mentioned as a suspect for taking steroids or human growth hormone to enhance his body. He simply trains harder than almost anyone else.

THE SCIENCE OF BASEBALL

Baseball is filled with science. The game is ruled by air resistance and gravity, temperature and humidity. Pitchers, batters, and fielders are all affected by air resistance. As a baseball pushes air aside after it has been pitched or hit, it loses energy and, therefore, it loses velocity. So, pitches and hits slow down. Physicist Robert Adair in *The Physics of Baseball* calculates that Cleveland Indian pitcher Bob Feller threw a ball that was going 98.6 miles per hour after it had traveled 60 feet. Since a pitch loses about 8 miles per hour from air resistance as it travels from the pitcher's hand to home plate, Feller's pitch was traveling about 107 miles per hour when it left his hand.

The stitches on the baseball help it cut through the air. If a baseball were smooth, it would travel a distance about 15 percent less than it would with stitches. Since a pitched curveball spins about 1,800 revolutions per minute, about the same as an electric motor, it can also move through the air as it curves. Gravity, though, takes it toll on pitches and hits. Pitched balls are always moving down when they cross home plate, as are batted balls when they leave the stadium. Thrown and batted balls, however, usually have backspin, which lifts the ball and holds it in the air longer, providing increased distance.

The speed of the bat as it travels through the hitting area is crucial to how far the ball goes. To hit an 85-mile-per-hour

1999: OVERCOMING HEARTBREAKING LOSSES

If the 1998 Yankees will be remembered as one of the best teams ever, the 1999 Yankees will be remembered as one that overcame more personal loss than any team should have to. Jeter's grandfather Sonny died of a heart attack in January 1999, and Jeter called that day one of the worst of his life. His beloved

fastball 400 feet, a bat must be traveling about 70 miles per hour when it makes contact. If a bat is traveling 80 miles per hour, the same ball would go about 450 feet. If 90 miles per hour, 500 feet. The ideal home run would be a 95-mile-per hour fastball pulled in 100-degree weather with a 20-mile-per hour wind helping it. It would travel about 530 feet at sea level, and 570 feet in Denver, Colorado, which is at an elevation of 5,280 feet, or one mile, above sea level.

Many aficionados argue about the longest home run. Most experts believe it was one hit by Mickey Mantle at Griffith Stadium in Washington, D.C., in 1953. The Yankees' publicity department said it traveled 565 feet. Adair calculates that it actually traveled about 506 feet. Some say a ball that Josh Gibson hit out of Yankee Stadium when he was playing for the Homestead Grays in the Negro League possibly traveled 520 feet. Mantle, Babe Ruth, Joe DiMaggio, and Lou Gehrig never hit a ball out of Yankee Stadium, but Gibson did, twice.

The ball can also be affected by temperature and humidity. Deep-freezing a ball to –10°F takes about 25 feet off a 375-foot fly ball. Warming a ball to 150°F adds about 25 feet. Since water vapor is lighter than air, a ball travels farther if the air is humid. Umpires are given the baseballs two hours before the game so they can be sure the balls have not been heated or cooled.

Yankee manager Joe Torre was diagnosed with prostate cancer during spring training, and he missed the first 36 games of the year to undergo chemotherapy and radiation. Teammate Darryl Strawberry battled colon cancer and drug addiction. The father of 1998 World Series MVP Scott Brosius died suddenly during the season, as did Luis Sojo's father. Pitcher Andy Pettitte's father became seriously ill. Another key player, Paul O'Neill, was told that his father had died suddenly of a heart attack, and O'Neill was visibly weakened by his grief.

Baseball teams spend a good deal of time together, and the players get to know one another throughout the long season. The personal tragedies made the team even closer. Somehow, they kept on winning baseball games and finished the season 98–64. The Yankees developed a reputation for playing their best from the seventh inning on, coming from behind so many times that people lost count. They made few errors, turned many double plays, and did not beat themselves with silly mistakes. They were not the powerful 1998 team that won their division by 22 games, but they won enough.

Jeter had the best year of his career. He got 219 hits, the most in the major leagues. He hit .349, with 70 extra-base hits. The season was one of the best any shortstop in baseball had ever had. He was only 25 years old, but he was playing with the wisdom and maturity of someone much older, growing up even faster because of all the personal tragedies around him.

He is always the "coolest cat in town," as Torre calls him. Just how cool he is was shown during a game on August 6, a Friday night in Seattle. The pitchers from both teams had been throwing at one another's hitters, and the game finally heated into a brawl, with players fighting all over the field. One Mariner, Alex Rodriguez, and one Yankee, Derek Jeter, refused to get caught up in the melee. They stood at the edges and warily watched each other. They were the two coolest heads on the field. A teammate later questioned why Jeter did not join the fight. Jeter describes his views on fighting:

> It's critical for me to show restraint. I get a lot of attention with the Yankees and, like other players, have to accept the fact that there are always going to be people who will want to harass me, tweak me, and try to rattle me. . . . I think it takes a bigger man to walk away from a problem than to stay and fight about it. What would you gain from fighting? It's nothing but trouble. If someone wants to be an idiot and wants to get into a fight with you, don't give him the satisfaction.

The Yankees not only endured the season, they prevailed. They won all of their postseason games except one, getting great pitching from Orlando Hernández, Mariano Rivera, David Cone, and new teammate Roger Clemens. The Yankees received timely hitting from many players, especially Jeter, who hit .375 in the postseason. They swept the Atlanta Braves in the World Series.

After the final game in Yankee Stadium, Jeter was surrounded by more than 200 reporters and dozens of photographers and TV camera operators in the clubhouse. All he wanted to do was find his father, his mother, and Sharlee in the chaos. He somehow spotted them waiting in a hallway near the famous Joe DiMaggio "Thank the Good Lord" sign. He hugged them tight and did not want to let go. "We squeezed each other, knowing what this amazing journey meant for us, acknowledging where it had all started, without saying a word. Our hugs were real tight. They spoke for us." This year more than any other must have made Jeter realize how much more important his family was than the camera lights, flashbulbs, and champagne.

2000: AN EXTRAORDINARY THREE-PEAT

Three World Championships in his first four years were not the only Jeter accomplishments that fans were talking about as he headed into the 2000 season. In his first four years, Jeter had 795 hits, which is more than Babe Ruth, Willie Mays, Ty

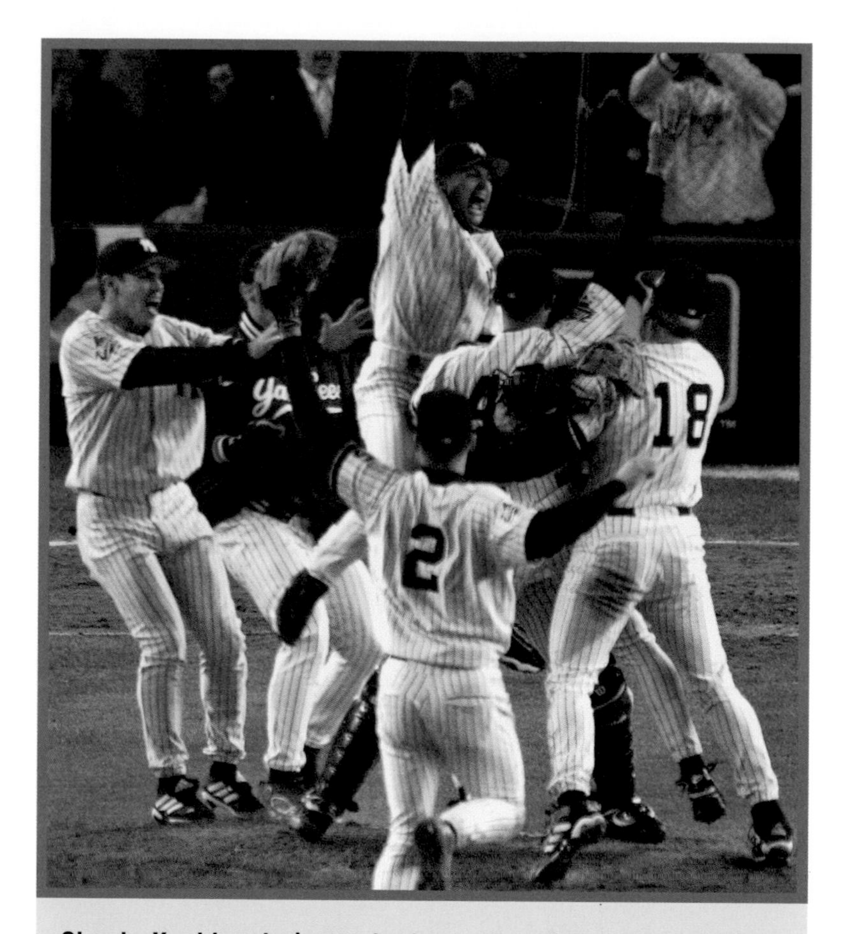

Chuck Knoblauch jumped above the heads of his teammates, including Derek Jeter *(foreground)*, as the Yankees celebrated their victory over the Atlanta Braves in the 1999 World Series. The 1999 team overcame much adversity, which made the players even closer.

Cobb, Pete Rose, and Hank Aaron had in their first four full seasons. Even though Jeter always gave credit to others, especially Yankee veterans like David Cone, Paul O'Neill, Bernie Williams, and Tino Martinez, he had for many fans become the Yankees' leader.

For the 2000 All-Star Game at Turner Field in Atlanta, Georgia, 51,317 fans turned out on a sweltering July night.

Charles, Dorothy, and Sharlee Jeter were there, hoping that Derek could do better than he had in his previous All-Star Game, when he struck out. Some have said that Jeter took a good amount of teasing from his family about that game. This night, there would be no teasing. Jeter had three hits and two RBIs and scored a run. He was named the game's Most Valuable Player, the first Yankee ever to win the award. A representative from the Baseball Hall of Fame took his black Louisville Slugger P72 bat back to Cooperstown.

When they reached the All-Star break, the Yankees had lost almost as many games as they had won, and they were behind the Toronto Blue Jays for first place in the American League East. Their two back-to-back World Series victories seemed a distant memory, and few felt they had a chance for a three-peat. Then, in early August, the team seemed to throw on a switch, and won 22 of 31 games. They beat and humbled the Boston Red Sox in Boston's Fenway Park on September 8, 9, and 10 and seemed back in control of their division. Then, they momentarily collapsed. Several key players, including Jeter, went into an end-of-season slump and the Yankees lost their last seven games by a combined score of 68-15. Some were worried that the team was tired. Jeter knew better—the team was simply waiting for the moments that counted, the playoffs and the World Series. "When it gets to September, I think guys just want to get September over with and get the playoffs started."

The Yankees beat the Oakland Athletics in the American League Division Series, three games to two. Pitcher Andy Pettitte saved them in the fifth game with a strong performance. They then beat the Seattle Mariners in the American League Championship Series, to face the New York Mets in the 2000 World Series, a "Subway Series." The Mets were not pushovers, losing their four World Series games by a total of five runs. Every game was close. When the Mets won Game 3, they stopped a Yankee winning streak in the World Series of 14 games. The Mets thought they had a chance to win it all going

After the Yankees beat the Mets in five games to win the 2000 World Series, Derek Jeter held up four fingers—to signify the four World Championships he and the Yankees had won since 1996.

into Game 4. When Jeter hit a home run on the first pitch of Game 4, the Mets seemed to sag, and soon the series would be over. Jeter hit another home run in the final game, batted .409 for the series, and was named the Most Valuable Player of the World Series. It was the first time that a player had been named MVP of the All-Star Game and the World Series in the same year. Jeter's year was a shining example of clutch hitting, of hitting when it mattered most. His fielding in the series was superb as well, and he was now approaching legendary status among his fans and teammates. He had done it all, and he was only 26.

The team took yet another ride down the Canyon of Heroes, for the fourth time in five years. A special float had been made for the World Series MVP, but Jeter refused to ride on it. He wanted to be with the other infielders, with his teammates and their families. He refused to be treated special, to be held above others. That parade on a cold late October day was the last time any celebrating team would see the World Trade Center towering over their party. For now, the 2000 Yankees could only enjoy their moment, and their leader could only wonder what the future would bring.

Slipping from Supremacy

In November 2000, Sharlee Jeter was attending Spelman College in Atlanta, Georgia. She took a nasty fall and went to the school infirmary when she felt lumps in her neck. The nurse said the injury was most likely a pulled muscle. When the lumps did not go away, Sharlee underwent a series of tests. She and her family were then told the bad news: Sharlee had a form of cancer called Hodgkin's disease.

Sharlee began chemotherapy treatments every two weeks. Her dream of being a softball player in the Olympics began to seem out of reach. She and her brother had always been close, but now they became even closer. They talked as often as five times a day. When a member of the family gets cancer, the whole family suffers. Seeing a loved one in pain, losing hair and worrying about life and death, each family member feels as if he or she is sick in some way as well.

Sharlee and the Jeters fought the disease with all they had. Sharlee went to New York City for some of her treatments and stayed in Atlanta for others. She reduced her course load but continued to take some classes as she worked her way toward a bachelor's degree in mathematics. She would not be able to graduate with her class, but suddenly that did not seem like the most important issue.

On a Friday in the middle of May, Sharlee came to Yankee Stadium to watch her brother play. She had good news. Her treatments had worked; tests showed no more sign of cancer. The family could now breathe again, and Jeter could begin to concentrate on baseball.

THE 2001 SEASON: HOPE AND TRAGEDY

Jeter did not just have Sharlee's illness to worry about as 2001 started. He was in the middle of the biggest contract negotiations of his career. Finally, in February, the Yankees agreed to pay him $189 million for 10 years, the second-richest contract in team-sports history. With his sister getting better and his contract disputes behind him, Jeter was ready for another extraordinary year. It would prove to be a year the world would never forget.

On Tuesday, September 11, 2001, four commercial airliners were hijacked, and two were flown into the World Trade Center. One was flown into the Pentagon in Arlington County, Virginia, and the fourth crashed into a field in Somerset County, Pennsylvania. The Yankees heard the news as America did, slowly and painfully. Suddenly, their season seemed both less and more important.

The Yankees team that had won three straight championships was good enough to win the American League pennant again. Time was taking its toll on the veterans, however, and everyone knew the Yankees were getting vulnerable. With the tragedy of 9/11, a city in shock turned to its beloved team for some distraction and relief.

The young Oakland A's were ready for the Yankees in the first round of the playoffs, and the A's won the first two games in the best-of-five series, at Yankee Stadium. The home fans were shocked. No team has ever lost the first two games of a short series at home and gone on to win, so as the A's flew to Oakland for Game 3, they must have felt confident that they were going to advance to the next round. In Game 3, Yankees pitcher Mike Mussina and A's pitcher Barry Zito were in a classic duel. The Yankees held onto a 1-0 lead in the bottom of the seventh inning, but Terrance Long of the A's slashed a ball just past the reach of Yankee first baseman Tino Martinez, and Jeremy Giambi headed home for what would be the tying run. Yankees right fielder Shane Spencer fielded the ball and let loose a wild throw toward home plate. The ball sailed over the head of the cut-off man, the player who is supposed to be able to catch it and relay it to home. The ball was so wild it flew over the head of the back-up cut-off man and seemed to be heading off the playing field.

Suddenly, out of nowhere, Jeter flew across the pitcher's mound, leapt into the air, caught the ball, and in one motion flipped the ball toward home plate and Jorge Posada, the Yankees catcher. Posada tagged Giambi out, and one of the most famous plays in postseason history became an instant classic. Teams simply don't practice having a third cut-off man make a play. Players had never seen a play like this one, nor, in all likelihood, will they ever again. ESPN lists "The Flip" as one of the most memorable sports moments of the past 25 years.

The Yankees became inspired, and the Athletics were shocked. The Yankees went on to win the game and the series. In the deciding Game 5, after getting his eighty-seventh career postseason hit (a new record), Jeter added another highlight. In the eighth inning, he dove into the photographers' box behind

Yankees catcher Jorge Posada *(right)* tagged out Jeremy Giambi on October 13, 2001, during Game 3 of the American League Division Series. Derek Jeter *(left)* had just caught a throw from right field that had sailed over the two cut-off men, and, in one motion, flipped the ball to Posada. The play, known as "The Flip," became an instant classic.

third base and caught a pop fly, cutting his elbow. The 54,642 fans in Yankee Stadium chanted his name.

The Yankees went on to win the American League Championship Series as well, defeating the Seattle Mariners four games to one. In a classic World Series, the Arizona Diamondbacks won the first two games in Arizona behind pitchers Curt Schilling and Randy Johnson. The Yankees won Games 3, 4, and 5 in Yankee Stadium, highlighted by a Jeter walk-off home run in the tenth inning of Game 4 on October 31. It was the first walk-off home run of his career, and it happened just after midnight, now on November 1, a Halloween present to all Yankees fans. Jeter was instantly nicknamed "Mr. November." When Scott Brosius hit a two-out, two-run homer in the ninth inning to tie Game 5, which the Yankees won in the twelfth inning, baseball historians began to call the series one of the best ever. In Game 7, Arizona scored two runs in the bottom of the ninth inning to win the championship. The Diamondbacks became the first team ever to rally from a ninth-inning deficit in Game 7 of a World Series. The home team won every game, and the country was treated to a brief break from tragic world events. The Yankees had not won, but in defeat they seemed even more sympathetic than if they had won.

2002 AND 2003: EXCELLENCE, BUT . . .

An era ended with the 2001 Yankees season. Even though they still had their star shortstop and several other key players, they lost more than any team could afford to and still stay at the very top. Paul O'Neill and Scott Brosius retired, and Tino Martinez and Chuck Knoblauch were lost to free agency. In 2002, Jeter hit .297, lower than his career average, and his slugging percentage and on-base percentage fell as well. He had only 44 extra-base hits, his lowest total as a Yankee.

As usual, Jeter had a strong postseason in 2002, but this time the playoffs ended quickly for the team. Jeter batted .500 against the Anaheim Angels in the American League Division Series, but for once he came up short in a crucial at-bat. In the second game, with the Yankees behind 8-6 in the eighth inning, Jeter came to bat with the bases loaded. Angel pitcher Troy Percival threw a 98-mile-per-hour (158-kilometer-per-hour) fastball, and Jeter swung and missed. After fouling off the next pitch, Jeter watched in disbelief as umpire Doug Eddings called strike three. No one could remember the last time Jeter

Yankees manager Joe Torre gave Derek Jeter a pat on the cheek on June 3, 2003, after Jeter was named captain of the team. The Yankees had not had a captain since Don Mattingly retired after the 1995 season.

had watched a third strike in a crucial postseason at-bat. For the first time in five years, the Yankees would be watching the World Series from home.

In December 2002, George Steinbrenner publicly criticized his star shortstop for a lack of focus, saying Jeter was staying out late too many nights. When Steinbrenner's comments hit the New York newspapers, Jeter was on vacation in Belize. When he returned home, he met with the owner behind closed doors. Jeter defended his work ethic and himself. Whatever was said that day, Steinbrenner was impressed enough with Jeter's handling of the criticism that, on June 3, 2003, he made Jeter the first captain of the Yankees since Don Mattingly retired in 1995. Steinbrenner said Jeter "represents all that is good about a leader. I'm a great believer in history, and I look at all the other

YANKEE CAPTAINS

No one is quite sure how many Yankee captains there have been. Some historians say as few as 11. Some say as many as 14. Certainly their two most famous ones were Babe Ruth, who was captain for only six games (in 1922), and Lou Gehrig, who was captain from 1935 to 1941. The first captain was probably Clark Griffith from 1903 to 1905, and the most recent one is Derek Jeter.

Being the captain is one of the most fabled honors in sports because of the rich Yankee tradition and the significance that Yankee ownership has placed on the leadership position. It has also been a subject of controversy, given how successful Yankee teams without captains have been. The team had no captain from 1926 to 1935, and during that time the Yankees won three World Championships. Many experts rate the 1927 Yankees as the best baseball team of all time. There was no captain from 1941 to 1976, and the Yankees won 12 World Series. The Yankees had no captain, as well, when they won their championships in 1996, 1998, 1999, and 2000.

Some have said that the captain's title carries a kind of curse. Only a few days after being named captain, Ruth had one

leaders down through Yankee history, and Jeter is right there with them." When the two made a Visa commercial together making fun of "The Flap," many Yankees fans breathed a sigh of relief.

The 2003 Yankees season had a bad start. On Opening Day in Toronto, Jeter dislocated his shoulder and had to sit out the first part of the season. He still managed to hit .324 in 119 games, with 10 home runs and 52 runs batted in, but experts

of the worst days of his baseball career; on May 22, 1922, Ruth uncharacteristically threw dirt at an umpire after being called out at second base and then went into the stands to attack a fan who called him a "bum." He was fined and suspended. Lou Gehrig died as Yankee captain, as did Thurman Munson, the captain from April 17, 1976, to August 2, 1979. Munson died in a small-plane crash while he was practicing takeoffs and landings at an airport near his home in Ohio.

Current New York Mets manager Willie Randolph was a Yankee captain from 1986 to 1989, and Yankee coach Don Mattingly was captain from 1991 to 1995. Those years were part of the long drought of championships, even though Randolph and Mattingly were among the best players in the league and the Yankees had strong teams in some of those years. As soon as the captain position was dissolved after 1995, the Yankees went on a championship winning streak. They have not won a World Championship since Jeter became captain in 2003. Superstition plays a big part in baseball, and the superstition about the "curse" of the Yankee captain lives on—at least until the Yankees win another World Championship with a captain.

believe that the injury slowed him all year. The Yankees won the pennant again, beating the Red Sox in a classic playoff series when Sox manager Grady Little left starting pitcher Pedro Martínez in Game 7 too long, allowing the Yankees to tie the game. New York won when Aaron Boone homered in the eleventh inning. The Yankees had made it back to the World Series, against the Florida Marlins, but the series with the Red Sox seemed to have taken too much effort. The Yankees lost to the upstart Marlins in six games. Instead of getting a hit just when they needed one, the Yankees appeared to come up a little short in crucial moments.

2004–2006: TIME FOR OTHERS TO WIN

The Yankees had now gone three years without a World Championship, and George Steinbrenner felt it was time to make a bold move. He signed Alex Rodriguez to play third base, adding the most expensive player in team sports to play next to Jeter, the second-most expensive player. The two had become close friends over the years, although the friendship cooled after Rodriguez told a magazine writer in 2001 that Jeter was not the main worry when teams faced the Yankees. Still, each thought that he was looking in a mirror when he watched the other.

The bitter rivalry between the Yankees and the Red Sox had heated up during the 2003 postseason and was going strong in 2004. In one of the most exciting regular-season games ever, the Yankees and Red Sox faced each other on July 1 in Yankee Stadium, fighting for first place. In the twelfth inning, Sox player Trot Nixon hit a fly ball that was about to drop in for a key hit when Jeter came from nowhere and caught it. He could not stop himself and crashed into the stands head first. He was dazed, and when he came out, he was bleeding from his face and chin. He looked as if he had been through a heavyweight fight. He was taken to Columbia-Presbyterian Hospital for stitches and X-rays, and the inspired Yankees won in the thirteenth inning.

The crowd at Yankee Stadium cheered as Derek Jeter was helped out of the stands after making a dramatic catch in the twelfth inning of a game against the Boston Red Sox on July 1, 2004. Jeter's momentum carried him into the stands, and he cut his face and chin.

The Red Sox went on to beat the Yankees in the 2004 American League Championship Series in one of the most famous baseball series ever played. The Red Sox lost the first three games of the series and were trailing by a run in the bottom of the ninth in Game 4. They won that game and the next three, becoming the first team ever to win a seven-game series after losing the first three games. The Sox went on to sweep the St. Louis Cardinals in the World Series. Yankees fans were in mourning, and some blamed the changed team dynamic with

Rodriguez as the new star. Others had fun with the Red Sox's breaking of "The Curse of the Bambino" (the Red Sox had not won a World Series after selling Babe Ruth to the Yankees) and said that the Yankees were now under the "Curse of Clay Bellinger." It seems that one of the players traded after 2000 was Clay Bellinger, and, of course, the team had not won a championship since. Some Yankees fans kept their sense of humor, even if others had not.

The Yankees celebrated the tenth anniversary of Jeter's arrival in the major leagues on May 29, 2005. The Yankee Stadium scoreboard flashed his accomplishments in his first 10 years: 1,793 hits, 1,073 runs scored, 155 home runs, 713 RBIs, a 2004 Gold Glove (awarded to the best fielder at each position), 6 All-Star Games, 6 World Series, and 4 World Championships. Even though 2005 would be another year without a World Championship—the Yankees lost to the Los Angeles Angels of Anaheim in the first round of the playoffs—Yankees fans remained as solidly behind their shortstop as they were when he helped win the 1996 World Series. Jeter had grown up with all of New York watching, and the city loved who he had become.

The Yankees' postseason skid continued in 2006, when they were eliminated in the Division Series by the Detroit Tigers. It was the second year in a row they went down in the first round. The fault was not Jeter's. He and Jorge Posada, the only two stars left from the Yankees' last champions, in 2000, both batted .500 in the Division Series. The rest of the team only batted .173.

Jeter's postseason matched his year overall—he had his best season of the decade, with a .343 batting average, 14 home runs, and 97 RBIs. He also won the Gold Glove. Still, his numbers were not enough to garner him his first American League Most Valuable Player award. Jeter finished second to Justin Morneau of the Minnesota Twins.

"You've heard me say it a thousand times, but winning the World Series for the New York Yankees continues to be my main focus," Jeter said in a statement after the MVP announcement. "There is no individual award that can compare with a championship trophy, and I look forward to working toward that challenge again in 2007."

The Continuing Inspiration

Derek Jeter has made his mark on many aspects of American life. His philanthropic work is famous. Every year around Christmas, children in New York hospitals are treated to a visit from Jeter. He comes with gifts donated to his Turn 2 Foundation, and he spends hours talking to the delighted youngsters. When he invites hundreds of kids to the Big Apple Circus in New York's Madison Square Garden, he jumps into the main ring and has as much fun as anyone.

When Jeter started the Turn 2 Foundation in his hotel room his rookie year, he could not have known that it would award more than $6 million in grants. Turn 2 helped create and support many kinds of programs, including "Jeter's Leaders," which recognizes students in New York City and Kalamazoo for both academic achievements and community service. "Turn 2 Us" is a healthy-lifestyle program partnering with the Children's Hospital of New York and Public School 128 in the Washington Heights section of Manhattan. "Turn 2 After School" reaches almost 400 children in New York with weekday activities in computer labs, visual arts, physical fitness, drama, and more. Baseball clinics, sports camps, scholarships, HIV/AIDS prevention programs, and drug and alcohol abuse prevention programs are all part of the Turn 2 Foundation. With Jeter and his father very active in all phases of the foundation, it is a model of how a famous athlete can multiply his or her forces for good.

HIS LOVE LIFE

Jeter admits in his autobiography, published in 2000, that he worries about whom he is going to marry. Many feel that his relationship with Mariah Carey was the most intense one of his life, but he has had several others. In May 2000, Jeter or his agent sent a Yankees ticket to Lara Dutta, who was then Miss Universe. A friendship and then a romance developed, and the pair was seen all over New York in the following months. On Election Night, in November 2000, they were in a trendy club until nearly dawn, perhaps waiting like the rest of the United States to see who the forty-third president would be. They enjoyed New York Knicks games, and many began to wonder if this relationship would become a serious one. It did not last, however.

In July 2002, gossip columns reported that Jeter and actress Jordana Brewster were dating. The Yale-educated star of *The Fast and the Furious* and Jeter were seen shopping and dining together for several months, but when Jeter was not at Brewster's twenty-sixth birthday party in April 2003, the tabloids speculated that the affair was over. After the 2003 season, Jeter was seen at a Knicks game with MTV host Vanessa Minnillo. She is a former Miss Teen USA and as rich and beautiful as any of the women in his life.

Mariah Carey and Derek Jeter, then a couple, attended a birthday party for Sean Combs in November 1998. Jeter has also dated former Miss Universe Lara Dutta, MTV personality Vanessa Minnillo, and actresses Jordana Brewster, Scarlett Johansson, and Jessica Alba.

The parade of beautiful women continued with actress Jessica Alba, someone Jeter had admired from a distance for many months and whom he met in California during a Yankee road trip in July 2004. He also reportedly had a few dates with actress Scarlett Johansson in December 2004. He has yet to settle into a long-term relationship with any of these stars, and he seems to be enjoying his bachelor status as much as any sports celebrity in memory.

A ROLE MODEL FOR ALL

Some people just see their lives as tied to the lives of others. They do not view themselves as rugged individualists who want to go it alone, but as members of many kinds of communities. These are people whom society needs to function—people who often do not get the attention they deserve for their social achievements. Jeter is the model of a healthy personality who somehow knew the purpose of his life was to discover his gifts and share those gifts with others. His gifts were not limited to baseball but included reaching out to others in a way that did not turn them off.

He was lucky enough and skilled enough to imagine the world he wanted to live in, and then live in it. Jeter looks past difficulties as if they are not there, or he wipes them out one by one. He finds situations that bring out the best in his own character and avoids those that do not. Many people believe that what happens to them determines who they are. People like Jeter believe who they are determines what happens to them.

Some have said that people with a biracial heritage have fewer limits on who they define as part of their ethnic group. Jeter has always been open-minded, open-hearted, extroverted, and agreeable. Biographer Patrick Giles describes this side of Jeter:

> It's been noted that among the swarms of young fans waiting for Jeter before and after games, many are like him: from

> more than one, sometimes several, races and ethnicities. With each generation, as Americans slowly relinquish the polarizations that blight our history, greater numbers of such children appear, often rejected or ignored by others. Such kids reach out to Derek not only because they admire his achievement but recognize in it, his all-accepting public manner . . . something of their own hoped-for futures.

Jeter knows what it feels like to be an outsider, and he has always tried to help others who feel the same way. He has been called an "Oreo" and a "zebra" because of his heritage. He

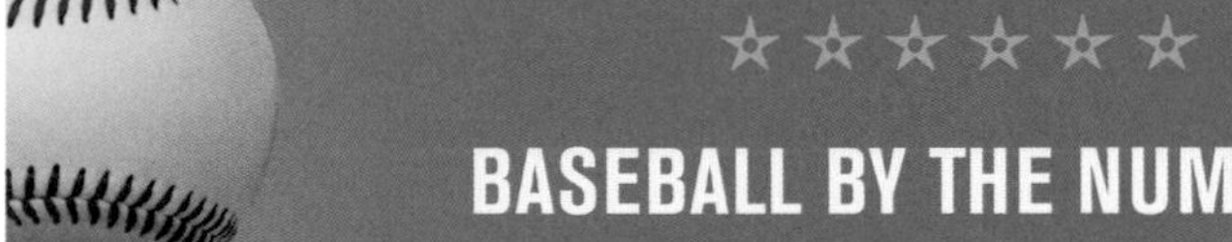

BASEBALL BY THE NUMBERS

One of the best aspects of baseball is that there are more statistics to keep track of than any other sport. There is some debate about what to count, however. In 1971, a small group of baseball fans interested in statistics started the "Society for American Baseball Research," or SABR. One of its leading figures was a man named Bill James, who made up the term *sabermetrics* for the study of baseball through new kinds of statistics. James showed that some baseball statistics confused luck and skill, and he wanted to find ways to rate players based more on skill than luck.

He and others in the sabermetric world noticed that a team's batting average was not a good predictor of whether a team won. Instead, on-base percentage (OBP) and slugging percentage (SLG) were keys to winning. On-base percentage (the number of times a player reaches base divided by the number of plate appearances) takes into account the importance of walks, which are ignored in batting average. Slugging percentage measures not just the number of hits divided by times at

chooses to call himself "black-and-white." He does not let others choose his identity. He chooses it for himself.

GOOD ADVICE

Jeter's autobiography is filled with good advice. He thinks that all good accomplishments start with goals. He tells his readers to ask themselves some very important questions just as early as they can: What do they love to do? What are they especially good at? Setting goals that are both dreams and future realities is one of the hardest tasks in life. Parents, teachers, and friends can help. For Jeter, his parents played a big role.

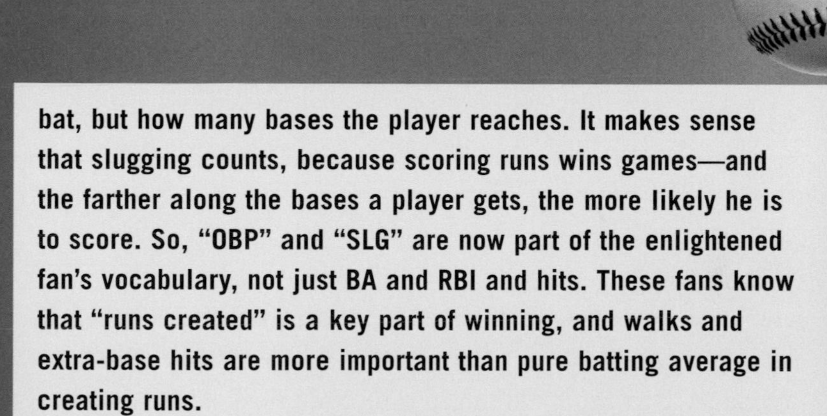

bat, but how many bases the player reaches. It makes sense that slugging counts, because scoring runs wins games—and the farther along the bases a player gets, the more likely he is to score. So, "OBP" and "SLG" are now part of the enlightened fan's vocabulary, not just BA and RBI and hits. These fans know that "runs created" is a key part of winning, and walks and extra-base hits are more important than pure batting average in creating runs.

This idea was shocking to most of the professional baseball world, which chose to ignore James and the new breed of baseball stat people for a long time. The "jocks" ignored the "nerds." Some still ignore them, but not the Oakland A's, Boston Red Sox, Los Angeles Dodgers, or Toronto Blue Jays. All those teams and some others are now making use of the "new" statistics when they evaluate players at all levels. The Red Sox hired James in 2002 and won a World Championship for the first time in 86 years in 2004. Coincidence?

The goals are not going to be easy. He warns his readers that they will fail and that they will feel pain. The world will not always be fair. But, if they have a passion for success, they will succeed. If they are afraid, and stay afraid, they will probably not succeed. If they look, listen, and learn, they will win. If they don't think before they act, they will lose.

Jeter's advice recognizes that life is not simple and has contradictions. Young people must be serious, but they also must have fun. They must be leaders, but they also must be followers. They need strong support from friends and family, but they have to rely on themselves as well. They need to be careful, but not be afraid of all risks. They need to be smart, but not just smart. He writes:

> I love being a positive person, so, although I stay focused and don't take things for granted, I don't sit around waiting for something bad to happen. That's unhealthy. I think you have to accept the fact that there are going to be new challenges for you every day and then go into that day believing you can overcome them. It works both ways. Bad days can follow good days—and vice versa.

HIS FUTURE

Jeter's contract runs through 2010, and he will be 36 when it ends. Will the Yankees re-sign him? Most think they will. Jeter is on a pace to get 3,500 hits, a milestone reached by very few players. There is little doubt that some day Jeter will join the other figures in Yankee Stadium's Monument Park. The statues of Babe Ruth, Lou Gehrig, Joe DiMaggio, and Mickey Mantle will have to make room for his likeness. Joe DiMaggio used to say that he played hard every day because there was always someone in the stands who had never seen him play before. Jeter feels exactly the same way. He is lucky enough to have joined a very rich tradition of Yankee stars. He has internalized that tradition and made it work for him.

After the Yankees won the 1999 World Series, Derek Jeter ran back to the clubhouse, passing under a sign that quotes Yankee legend Joe DiMaggio. Jeter himself has secured an important place in Yankee history.

Shortstops have rarely played past 40 years old, and Jeter will be 40 in 2014. Given his nature, he will almost certainly retire before his skills become severely diminished. When he takes the last walk under the DiMaggio sign and touches it for the last time, he will be remembered as a brilliant player who had a great deal of success early in his career, and probably late in his career as well. He has touched so many lives, young and old, white and black and Hispanic and Asian, that he will be remembered as long as baseball is played.

STATISTICS

DEREK JETER

Primary position: Shortstop

Full name: Derek Sanderson Jeter • Born: June 26, 1974, Pequannock, New Jersey • Height: 6'3" • Weight: 195 lbs. • Team: New York Yankees (1995–present)

YEAR	TEAM	G	AB	H	HR	RBI	BA
1995	NYY	15	48	12	0	7	.250
1996	NYY	157	582	183	10	78	.314
1997	NYY	159	654	190	10	70	.291
1998	NYY	149	626	203	19	84	.324
1999	NYY	158	627	219	24	102	.349
2000	NYY	148	593	201	15	73	.339
2001	NYY	150	614	191	21	74	.311
2002	NYY	157	644	191	18	75	.297
2003	NYY	119	482	156	10	52	.324
2004	NYY	154	643	188	23	78	.292
2005	NYY	159	654	202	19	70	.309
2006	NYY	154	623	214	14	97	.343
TOTALS		1,679	6,790	2,150	183	860	.317

Key: NYY = New York Yankees; G = Games; AB = At-bats; H = Hits; HR = Home runs; RBI = Runs batted in; BA = Batting average

CHRONOLOGY

1974 **June 26** Born in Pequannock, New Jersey.

1978 Charles, Dorothy, and Derek Jeter move to Kalamazoo, Michigan.

1979 Begins to play T-ball.

1980 Attends his first Yankee game with his grandmother, while visiting his grandparents in New Jersey.

1984 The Jeters move into a new home behind Kalamazoo Central High School, giving Derek more fields on which to practice.

1988 Graduates from St. Augustine School in Kalamazoo, and his yearbook states his goal of becoming a Yankee.

TIMELINE

1974 Born in Pequannock, New Jersey

1980 Attends his first Yankee game with his grandmother

1989 Starts for his varsity baseball team as a freshman

1991 Hits .557 with seven home runs as a high school junior

1992 Named *USA Today*'s High School Player of the Year and is drafted by the Yankees

1993 Voted "Most Outstanding Major League Prospect" by South Atlantic League managers

1995 Makes his major-league debut at Seattle

1974 — 1995

1989 Starts for the varsity baseball team at Kalamazoo Central High School as a freshman.

1991 Hits .557 with seven home runs as a high school junior and is scouted by most major-league teams.

1992 Hits .508 as a senior and is named *USA Today*'s High School Player of the Year

June 1 Drafted sixth by the New York Yankees; reports to Tampa, Florida, to play in the Gulf Coast Rookie League, and then attends the University of Michigan for a term in the fall.

1993 Voted "Most Outstanding Major League Prospect" by South Atlantic League managers after hitting .295

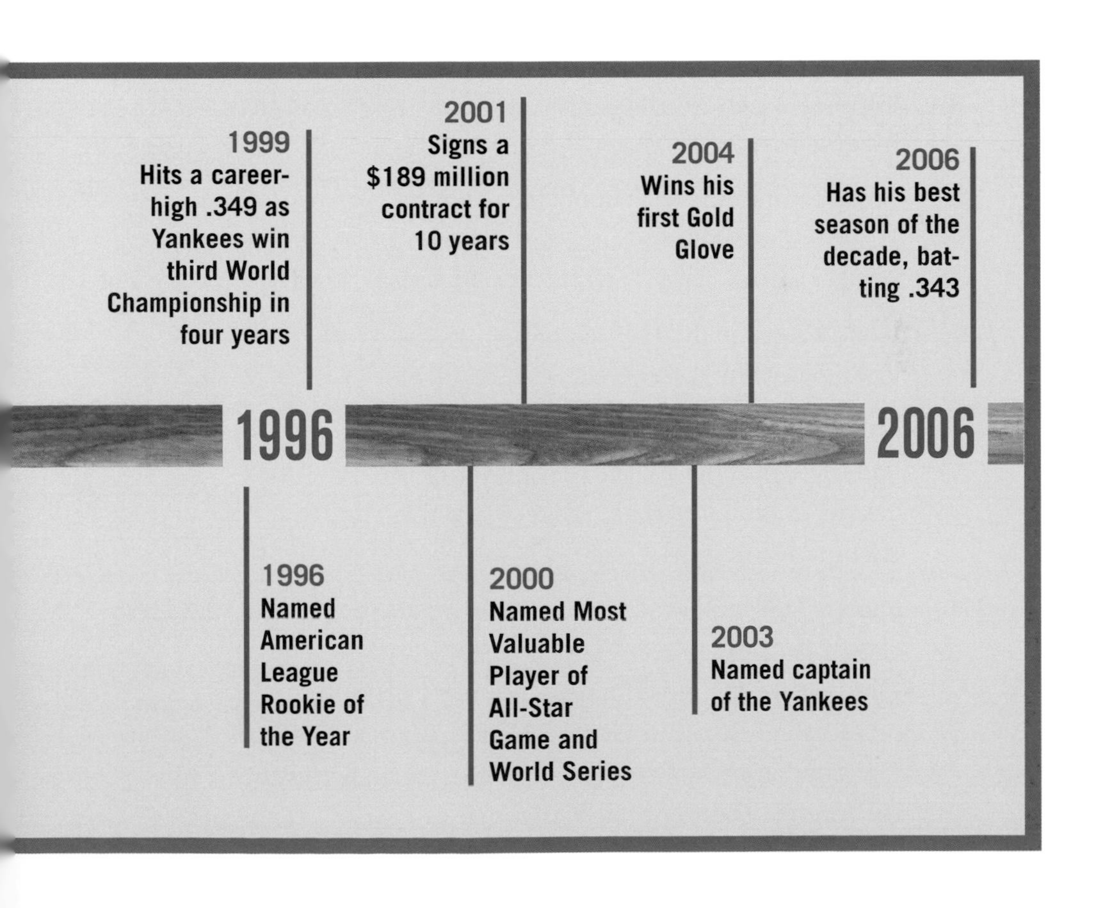

with 5 home runs, 71 runs batted in, and 18 stolen bases at Class-A Greensboro.

1994 Voted Minor League Player of the Year by *Baseball America.*

1995 **May 29** Makes his major-league debut at Seattle when Yankee shortstop Tony Fernández is placed on the disabled list.

May 30 Gets his first major-league hit and scores his first run.

1996 Becomes Yankee shortstop full time, and on Opening Day hits a home run; finishes year with .314 average and is named American League Rookie of the Year; Yankees win World Series, and Jeter bats .361 in postseason; starts the Turn 2 Foundation.

November Meets Mariah Carey at a fund-raiser and they become friends.

1998 Voted to first All-Star Game; bats .324 for season, with 203 hits and 19 home runs; Yankees win a record 125 regular-season games and the World Series.

1999 Hits a career-high .349; Yankees win third World Championship in four years.

2000 Named Most Valuable Player of both the All-Star Game and the World Series, the first player ever to win both awards in the same year; Yankees win their fourth championship in five years.

2001 Signs a $189 million contract for 10 years, the second-richest contract in team-sports history; makes "The Flip," one of the most famous defensive plays in postseason history, in Game 3 of the American League Division Series; Yankees lose a classic World Series to the Arizona Diamondbacks in seven games.

2002 Yankees lose to Anaheim Angels in American League Division Series, but Jeter bats .500 for the series; George Steinbrenner publicly criticizes him for staying out late too many nights in New York.

2003 **June 3** Named captain of the Yankees, the first since Don Mattingly retired in 1995.

2004 Wins his first Gold Glove, voted on by players and managers and awarded by Rawlings for defensive excellence; Yankees lose a classic American League Championship Series to Red Sox in seven games.

2005 **May 29** Yankees celebrate his tenth anniversary; in first 10 years, he has 1,793 hits, 1,073 runs, 155 home runs, and 713 RBIs.

2006 Has his best season of the decade, batting .343; finishes second in voting for American League MVP.

GLOSSARY

at-bat (AB) An official turn at batting that is charged to a baseball player, except when the player walks, sacrifices, is hit by a pitched ball, or is interfered with by a catcher.

base on balls When a batter receives four pitches out of the strike zone, the batter receives a base on balls, also called a "walk," and goes to first base.

batter's box The area to the left and right of home plate in which the batter must be standing for fair play to resume.

batting average The number of hits a batter gets divided by the number of at-bats. For example, 3 hits in 10 at-bats would be a .300 batting average.

bunt A ball not fully hit, with the batter either intending to get to first base before the infielder can field the ball, or allowing an existing base runner to advance a base.

cut-off man A fielder who "cuts off" a long throw to an important target. Often the shortstop or second baseman is the cut-off man for a long throw from the outfield to third base or home plate.

designated hitter In the American League, a player who bats each time for the pitcher. There is no designated hitter in the National League. Baseball is the only professional sport in which different rules apply in different sections of the league. The lack of consistency in the use of the designated hitter is an ongoing debate.

double play A play by the defense in which two offensive players are put out in a continuous action.

dugout The area where the players and managers not on the field can wait and watch. It usually has a bench with a roof, and in the major leagues includes a baseball bat rack, glove and towel holders, a water cooler, a telephone to the bullpen, and more.

earned-run average (ERA) The average number of runs a pitcher allows per nine-inning game; the runs must be scored without errors by defensive players.

error The game's scorer designates an error when a defensive player makes a mistake that results in a runner reaching base.

fair ball A ball hit between the two foul lines that run down first base and third base to the stands and beyond. Fair territory is the part of the playing field between the first- and third-base foul lines, extending into the stands and beyond. The foul lines themselves are in fair territory.

foul ball A batted ball that lands in foul territory, which is the part of the playing field that is outside the first- and third-base foul lines.

grand slam A home run with three runners on base, resulting in four runs for the offensive team. The grand slam is one of the most dramatic plays in baseball.

home run When a batter hits a ball into the stands in fair territory, it is a home run. The batter may also have an inside-the-park home run if the ball never leaves the playing field and the runner is able to reach home plate without stopping before being tagged by a defensive player. A home run counts as one run, and if there are any runners on base when a home run is hit, they too score.

on-base percentage (OBP) The number of times a player reaches base divided by the number of plate appearances.

on deck The offensive player next in line to bat after the current batter is said to be on deck. Often the player on deck will swing a weighted bat to warm up and stay in an area called the on-deck circle.

opposite-field hit A hit to the opposite side of the field from the direction of a player's swing. For example, a left-handed batter would hit to left field and a right-handed batter would hit to right field.

perfect game A very rare no-hitter during which each batter is consecutively retired, allowing no base runners via walks, errors, or other means.

runs batted in (RBI) The number of runs that score as a direct result of a batter's hit(s) are the runs batted in by that batter. The major-league record is 191 RBIs for a single year by one batter.

sabermetrics The study of baseball using nontraditional statistics. Traditional baseball-performance measurement focuses on batting average, hits, home runs, and earned-run average. Sabermetrics tries to measure those statistics that predict winning and losing most accurately. On-base percentage and slugging percentage are two key sabermetric statistics.

slugging percentage (SLG) The number of bases a player reaches divided by the number of at-bats. It is a measure of the power of a batter.

strike zone The area directly over home plate up to the batter's chest (roughly where the batter's uniform lettering is) and down to his or her knees. Different umpires have slightly different strike zones, and players only ask that they be consistent.

tag The act of a defensive player touching a runner with his glove or hand while the defensive player is in possession of the ball. The runner is out when tagged.

umpire The official who rules on plays. For most baseball games, a home-plate umpire calls ball and strikes, and another umpire in the infield rules on outs at bases.

walk-off home run A game-ending home run by the home team—so named because the losing team has to walk off the field.

BIBLIOGRAPHY

Adair, Robert K. *The Physics of Baseball.* 3rd ed. New York: HarperCollins, 2002.

Curry, Jack. "Jeter Fails, For a Change, In October." *New York Times,* October 3, 2002.

———. "Jeter Gives the Fans an All-Star Performance." *New York Times,* July 12, 2000.

———. "To Understand Success of Jeter, Calm Down." *New York Times,* October 7, 2003.

Deveney, Sean. "Forging a Special Bond." *Sporting News,* December 13, 1999.

Donovan, Sandy. *Derek Jeter.* Minneapolis, Minn.: Lerner Publishing Group, 2004.

Frisch, Aaron. *Derek Jeter.* Mankato, Minn.: Creative Education, 2004.

Giles, Patrick. *Derek Jeter: Pride of the Yankees.* New York: St. Martin's Press, 1998.

Grossfield, Stan. "Blast From the Past." *Boston Globe,* April 19, 2006.

Jeter, Derek, with Jack Curry. *The Life You Imagine: Life Lessons for Achieving Your Dreams.* New York: Three Rivers Press, 2000.

Kepner, Tyler. "Jeter Gives Another Clinic in Leadership." *New York Times,* July 3, 2004.

———. "Steinbrenner Appoints Jeter Captain of the Yankees." *New York Times,* June 4, 2003.

Ladson, William. "The '98 Yankees: The Greatest Season, but Not the Greatest Team." *Sporting News,* November 2, 1998.

Lewis, Michael. *Moneyball: The Art of Winning an Unfair Game.* New York: W.W. Norton, 2003.

FURTHER READING

Christopher, Matt. *On the Field With . . . Derek Jeter.* New York: Little, Brown, 2000.

Donovan, Sandy. *Derek Jeter.* Minneapolis, Minn.: Lerner Publishing Group, 2004.

Giles, Patrick. *Derek Jeter: Pride of the Yankees.* New York: St. Martin's Press, 1998.

Harper, John, and Bob Klapisch. *Champions!* New York: Villard Books, 1996.

King, George. *Unbeatable! The Historic Season of the 1998 World Champion New York Yankees.* New York: HarperCollins, 1998.

Stout, Glenn. *Yankees Century: 100 Years of New York Yankees Baseball.* Boston, Mass.: Houghton Mifflin, 2002.

Vancil, Mark, and Mark Mandrake. *The Greatest Yankees Teams.* New York: Ballantine Books, 2004.

WEB SITES

Baseball Almanac
http://www.baseball-almanac.com

Baseball Reference
http://www.baseball-reference.com

Little League Online
http://www.littleleague.org

MLB.com (the official site of Major League Baseball)
http://mlb.mlb.com/index.jsp

New York Yankees
http://newyork.yankees.mlb.com

The Official Site of Derek Jeter
http://www.derekjeter.com

PICTURE CREDITS

PAGE

2: AP Images
7: Getty Images
11: AP Images
18: MLB Photos via Getty Images
23: AP Images
25: AP Images
30: AP Images
33: Getty Images
44: Diamond Images/ Getty Images
46: AP Images
50: Diamond Images/ Getty Images
55: AP Images
60: Getty Images
62: AP Images
68: Getty Images
73: AP Images
75: AP Images
82: AP Images
84: AP Images
89: AP Images
91: AP Images
95: Getty Images
100: Time & Life Pictures/ Getty Images
105: AP Images
107: AP Images

COVER

© Ray Stubblebine/Reuters/Landov

INDEX

ABOUT THE AUTHOR

CLIFFORD W. MILLS is a writer and editor living in Jacksonville, Florida. He has written biographies of Pope Benedict XVI and Virginia Woolf, compiled a volume of essays about J. D. Salinger, and has worked as an editor for John Wiley and Sons and Oxford University Press. He played baseball in college and had dreams of playing third base for the Yankees.